*A Correspondence Between Two Dutchmen – son Max
and father, Philip Kohnstamm*

1938–1939

STILL NO WAR

Edited by Dolph Kohnstamm

ATHENA PRESS
LONDON

First Published 2003 by
ATHENA PRESS
Queen's House, 2 Holly Road
Twickenham TW1 4EG
United Kingdom

The Dutch edition of this correspondence
was published by Amsterdam University Press,
October 2001

Printed for Athena Press

STILL NO WAR

Compiled and edited by Dolph Kohnstamm, Emeritus professor of Leiden University, Holland.

Revised and translated by Helen Richardson Borkent.

Foreword by Geert Mak, University Chair,
Amsterdam University

A young Dutch student writes letters to his parents – and some sixty years later, we read them with fascination and without interruption. What is going on?

In the first place, there is the trip that the young Max Kohnstamm is taking – a voyage through the America of the Depression, of the Negro question, of Roosevelt, of the New Deal. There are the encounters he has, told with a freshness and candor – a meal with the great Ernie Pyle, for example, in which he has no idea whatsoever of this legendary journalist's authority.

Second, there is his perspective, the perspective of a well-bred, well-educated fraternity student confronted for the first time with the reality of simultaneous poverty and a superiority in America. It is also the view of a pre-war Dutchman, who is getting a taste of a wave of prosperity that will not reach the Netherlands for a quarter of a century.

And third, there is the moment in time in which this trip takes place: during the final year of freedom, the ten months between the Munich Agreement and the last attempts to avert the German invasion of Poland. Holland was sleeping, it is said of that period, but these letters lend nuance to that image. Both Kohnstamms knew very well what was going on. Every move is noted and commented upon – often, aptly, in the light of what was to come. And it is not just their awareness of the approaching war that is important; Philip Kohnstamm is even able to look beyond the war. From a speech of Roosevelt, he immediately deduces its essential message: the President's intention to support the European democracies. And he is clearly relieved. He is certain, already in the winter of 1938–39, that the coming war will be won, no matter how difficult it may become.

But there is something else that makes this correspondence so fascinating to read. That is the time, the color, the intellectual ambiance in which these letters are written. When a homesick Max on a wintry day in Washington nostalgically describes in a few shining sentences a train ride from Amsterdam to the village where his parents live, the contemporary reader can only think: this Amsterdam, this Holland, no longer exists. The same feeling also arises in reading the discussions between father and son: here is an intellectual world, a sort of Dutch burgher society that has almost disappeared. I cannot describe it very well, this combination of Protestant religious idealism, the old debate culture of the Amsterdam student clubs, the intellectual tradition in families of Jewish ancestry and the erudite climate of the University of Amsterdam. But whatever it is, it makes these letters a small, unexpected and invaluable treasure.

Geert Mak

Max Kohnstamm

Introduction

October 1938. A young Dutchman named Max Kohnstamm, a student of history at the University of Amsterdam, sails to New York. He is still angry over the Munich Agreement, signed on September 29, between Hitler, Mussolini, Chamberlain (UK) and Daladier (France). He does not believe in appeasement. He fears the worst.

Max has received a small grant from American University in Washington DC, at that time specifically a school for government employees, where he hopes to learn more about Roosevelt's New Deal.

He begins writing letters home, and his parents and friends reply – by slow mail. A letter takes on average ten days to cross the Atlantic and reach its destination. His father Philip, a professor of education at the University of Amsterdam with many contacts in the United States, provides him with introductions to helpful colleagues.

November 1938. *Kristallnacht* or the Night of Broken Glass. Violent pogroms sweep across Germany and Austria on the nights of November 9 and 10. Max's sister and her children are still living in Germany. Friends of Max in Amsterdam are actively engaged in helping Jews to flee Germany.

Max buys a second-hand roadster for $150. Determined to see how the New Deal works in practice, he sets out in January 1939 to visit the South. In Virginia, North Carolina, Georgia, Alabama and Tennessee he talks with government officials and ordinary people, black and white. His letters home bear witness to his indignation at the exploitation of tenant farmers, racism, poverty and the devastation of once fertile soil. Both charmed and shocked by the South, he returns to New York, convinced that the United States cannot legitimately come to Europe's rescue from dictatorship until it has set its own house in order. His father, a wise man, tries in his letters to placate Max. Philip is convinced that a war is inevitable, that it is the only way to stop Hitler and his allies from controlling Europe, but also, that a war can only be won with America's help. He also holds America responsible for the detrimental consequences of the World War I peace treaty, signed in Versailles.

Throughout the spring and early summer Max continues his exploratory mission, traveling to the North-east – to Yale University in New Haven and Boston – and then west to Detroit, Chicago, Madison (Wisconsin) and finally Iowa. His original intention to go all the way to the West Coast, to visit a girlfriend from Washington at her parent's home in California, ends in grief. He abruptly changes plans and heads back to Washington. By this time his longing for home and the Netherlands, notwith-standing the ominous situation there and knowing that he could soon be lying in the trenches, compels him to sell his faithful two-seater and book passage home.

August 1939. The SS *Washington* sails for Europe. Aboard is a young man whose thoughts and perceptions have focused his life forever. A war will come but he looks ahead to peace. Only the stars can foresee the role he will play one world war and one decade later in the pacification and uniting of the European adversaries.

This small volume is a compilation of the letters written by Max to his parents, and the replies he received from his father. Max addressed most of his letters to his mother, taking for granted that they would of course be read by his father, and by the many visitors to their home. Some of the letters were directly addressed to his father. The letters written by Max's mother have appeared in a separate and private Dutch edition. Very little was omitted from the letters by Max's father, more from those written by his son. Selections were based on criteria of interest for a reader unacquainted with the details of daily life in this particular family, or of local pre-war Dutch politics and circumstances. The decisions to omit passages were mine, as a nephew of Max and grandson to Philip. Max authorized both the selections and the translation made by Helen Richardson Borkent, an American editor living in Amsterdam.

The order of the letters is chronological, to the extent that this is possible. Sometimes letters crossed at sea and often Max would write a subsequent letter before his father had responded to an earlier one.

Two Dutch careers

Philip A. Kohnstamm (1875–1951) was a distinguished professor of education at the University of Amsterdam, the Netherlands. He began his career as a professor of thermodynamics, in the same department as his tutor, the physicist and Nobel laureate, Diederik van der Waals. Gradually, Kohnstamm saw his interests change from physics to philosophy and theology and finally to education. The main building of the faculty of education of the University of Amsterdam bears his name.

A son of Jewish parents, he joined the Dutch Reformed Church in 1917. In 1903 he married An Kessler, the eldest daughter of J.B.A. Kessler, founder of Royal Dutch Petroleum Company, now the Royal Dutch/Shell Group. He was among the first in the Netherlands to do empirical research in education, focusing on the transfer of acquired insights. In the years before World War II he wrote articles defending democracy against totalitarianism and analyzing the roots of anti-Semitism. His mar

Philip Kohnstamm (1875-1951)

riage to a non-Jewish woman, together with his prominence in the Dutch Reformed Church, saved him from deportation by the Nazis. Both his sisters, however, died in Auschwitz. He, together with all professors of Jewish descent, was forced to leave the university in 1940. Resuming his academic position in 1945, he retired one year later at age 71 but continued to work in an advisory capacity.

Very few of his publications were translated into English. Two of his articles appeared in *The Personalist*, a philosophical quarterly of the University of Southern California at Lost Angeles, in 1937 and 1939.

Max Kohnstamm (1914–), the youngest son of Philip Kohnstamm and An Kessler, was born in Amsterdam. He studied history at the University of Amsterdam and in his fourth year, 1938–1939, traveled to the United States on a small grant from American University in Washington DC to broaden his historical and political views. The correspondence published here, between Max and his father, dates from this pre-war period in America.

From 1942 to 1944 Max was imprisoned by the Nazis in the Netherlands, first in a concentration camp and later in a detention camp for prominent Dutch hostages. In 1944 he married Kathleen Sillem, his present wife. When the war ended in 1945, Queen Wilhelmina, returned from exile in London, appointed him as one of her two personal secretaries, and he served her until her abdication in 1948. Max then entered the Dutch Foreign Office and in 1952 became Secretary of the Commission of the European Coal and Steel Community, the first institution of the organization that led to the formation of the Common Market of the European Union. In 1956 Jean Monnet, one of the founding fathers of the European Union, appointed Max Secretary-general of his Action Committee of the United States of Europe, a position he held until 1975.

In 1976 Max became the first President of the European University Institute in Florence, Italy, retiring in 1981. Living in Brussels and the Belgian Ardennes, he has remained a tenacious advocate for Europe up to the present day, inspired by the visionary ideas of Jean Monnet.

Dolph Kohnstamm, Amsterdam, Fall 2002

We entered New York harbor very late at night on the 25th. And what a magnificent entry it was. A fairy-tale city, the skyscrapers rising up into the dark night, defined by their illuminated windows. It was impressive. After much fuss and bother with visa control and customs, I finally found myself alone on the pier. I made my way easily by bus to the YMCA's Sloane House, where I obtained a good room with a view of the city.

I stayed in New York until the following evening. Nothing of real interest at the Institute of International Education. But the beauty of the city came as a complete surprise. I had expected great size and technical wizardry but not that the city would be so astonishingly beautiful. When I walked out onto the terrace atop the Empire State Building, from which you can see all of Manhattan, I was overcome by a sense of awe. What lay before me was a supreme human achievement. The setting sun, the Hudson, the ships, Wall Street, the Statue of Liberty – all the shapes of the city. Comparable perhaps to illustrations of Persian and Assyrian cities.

New York also has something friendly about it, something welcoming. I felt none of the frantic pace I had expected. The city was busy, naturally, but you can get around fine on foot. It was not even very noisy. Easy to find your way around. And then the port! There is not a street in Manhattan from which you cannot see something of the sea. There is a feeling of openness that Paris and London lack. You keep hearing the ships and catching glimpses of the water. The Battery, on the water and close to Wall Street, is beautiful: a quiet, sunny, and peaceful park at the edge of the immense harbor opening out to the whole world. And when you have finished gazing out over the glittering blue waves, you turn around and there it is – the majestic splendor of Manhattan.

[...]

In the afternoon I tried to find my way to Van Cortland Park by subway, also a good means to view the city. It was only then, during the endless ride to 140th Street, passing through one neighborhood after another, that I felt for the first time something of the angst in the relentless, merciless concrete desert. I long to see it once again. But at that moment my impression was not of Manhattan, open to sky and sea, but of a vast and threatening hinterland.

I am now living at 1306 21st Street N.W. in Washington in a house with six American students, most of whom are studying and working at the same time. They are very compatible and I am happy to be living among Americans instead of Chinese, Brazilians, Scandinavians, etc. [as would have been the case in the always fully-booked International House]. Up to now the financial side of things has been insufficient to poor. In addition, life here is very expensive. A dollar is worth a guilder… and not one cent more.[1] This is the situation: you need at least $80–100 a month to live. The American University provides me with at most $35–40. The International House – where I continue to take my meals – provides a few contacts but is far too international to be of any importance to me. Because the American University trains people for the civil service, it also provides a few contacts and some interesting lectures. But it leaves me very free, and that means I have no advisor for my studies here. In short, my trump cards are a little money, a few contacts and absolute freedom. In addition, the Library of Congress, the Government, union headquarters, the first US Negro university, and the first US Catholic university. What I miss is a first-rate college life and above all, an advisor.

What to do now? It would have been good if I had written a thesis in Holland and come here to finish it. But I didn't. One possibility: I can write a doctoral dissertation here on some aspect of American history. But I did not come here to do that. Second possibility: leave immediately. Admit that I have taken the wrong course and let Sloane Coffin take me under his wing.[2] Advantages

---

1. The official exchange rate at that time was 1.84 Dutch guilders to one US dollar.
2. Henry Sloane Coffin, American Presbyterian clergyman and president of Union Theological Seminary in New York City from 1926 to 1945.

would be an advisor, and thus an efficient use of my time. Disadvantages would be the cost, but even more important, the retreat: surrendering to what are indeed no small difficulties lying between me and an interesting year.

This said, I propose the following plan of action. College life vs freedom. I can experience college life here at the much larger George Washington University. If I make the most of the American University faculty and a few older students, I can try to orient myself regarding American's problems as fast as possible. In addition, I can learn English, and pursue contacts with the Negro university, Catholics and the labor unions. These ought to be three very important factors of American life. At the same time, I can get to know the city and seek to meet young New Deal people. I would then spend the Christmas holidays in New York and via Sloane Coffin gain some insight into the role of Protestantism in American society and think about what to do next. In short, until January 10 or thereabouts, I propose not to begin any specific study, using the time instead as a period of orientation. [...]

Questions remain: does Father agree with this plan of action? The risk is that I waste six weeks and $120. What is Father's opinion with regard to finances for this year? How heavily must I weigh that? I long to hear from you about this. It could be that I am too hasty in my conclusions and will look at things differently in two weeks. But writing back and forth takes so much time that I feel this plan is the best way to straighten things out by Christmas. […]

Ermelo,
November 16, 1938

Dear Son,
It seems to me that American University must be a big disappointment for you. My feeling is that under these circumstances, I would drastically curtail the duration of my US trip unless an opportunity can be found elsewhere to study and experience American spiritual life more in accordance with the original objective. You could turn for advice to […] Walter Kotschnig.[3] He would jump at the chance to have you spend the Christmas holidays with him. He lives in a small university town, about two hours by train from New York. I am no judge of whether you will find what you are looking for there but I think you will feel at home.

I also think that Walter has a great many connections and has looked round America with just those eyes of an educated European, making an introduction to him well worth your while.

Your description of New York has affected me deeply. It is the first time I have seen such emphasis placed on one's aesthetic impressions of the city. But I won't go into that now. I have had to postpone answering your letter several times because of so much dictating to do and I am determined to post my reply today.

Very much love,
Father

---

3. Walter M. Kotschnig, friend of Philip Kohnstamm and a professor at Smith College and Mount Holyoke College in Massachusetts from 1938 to 1942. An authority on international organization, he became a member of the US State Department in 1944. In the 1950s he represented the United States in the United Nations.

Dear Mother and Father,
The *Nieuw Amsterdam* sails tomorrow and I must send you a few words. Thank you for your letter, Mother. It is a very rich feeling to find a letter in the postbox.

[...]

America races over me like a hurricane. The impressions are so many and so varied, so confusing and so difficult to evaluate that again this week you must not expect a long account from me. If this continues, you will have to reserve the whole month of my return to listen to my stories. My impressions and moods fluctuate widely. I will give you two extreme examples:

– Where is Europe? Is there nowhere anything familiar? This could be Mars. What is happening here is indescribably important and incomprehensibly new. I live among people who are superbly educated, and with an unprecedented courage and unprecedented power are building a state that bears as little resemblance to our capitalist society as Russia does. The difficulties are enormous, the dangers are great, but the commitment to the struggle makes life here more fascinating than anywhere else in the world. The New Society, if it is to be built anywhere, will be built here.

– If only these uncouth loudmouths would shut up for just two minutes! I would give ten years of my life to see their radios, refrigerators, cars, lifts, and drugstores piled up into a big heap and set on fire. And ten more to see a universal ban on the use of American English. Then I will settle for a beautiful old house with beautiful things in it, books, Jaap and you.[4] If one more rude American uses the expression 'standard of living' one more time, I am going to do something very drastic.

[...]

In the first instance, I am buoyed by the lectures, the Library of Congress, the government buildings, the hours well spent with books, newspapers, journals and people. The second instance is linked to my bare and rather sad bedroom which, by virtue of two

---

4. Jaap Kalff, close friend of Max.

chairs and a sort of writing table, doubles as my sitting room. The fact is that the house where I live is about as uninviting as you can get, certainly in terms of furniture, lighting, etc. But the people – all students who hold government jobs – are delightful, interesting as well as very interested, educated and very well informed about Europe. If only they would not carry on loud conversations or, worse, yawn when their radios are broadcasting Toscanini.

To reiterate the pros and cons of American University and my stay here: the working environment is good and the lectures are better than I had expected. It is hard to explain but the strange old building in which the university is housed seems to suit the surroundings and says absolutely nothing about the quality of the faculty, which is first-class. The university is – in short – New Deal, only without funds, but so are other parts of the New Deal, for that matter. It is young, a bit wild, maybe even out of control. Most people are connected with the Government in one way or another. Professors run things and students play a minor role. Everybody is very busy and has little time for you. […]

A few other points. The dimensions – the sheer size – of everything here make it unbelievably difficult not to be taken in by them, not to be pulled into adjusting your own standards to conform to the American ones. You must constantly be on guard not to be misled by sizes and numbers and figures. An example: if the Library of Congress – given the same ratios – were smaller, it would be kitsch and hilariously funny. But it is not small and I walk through it like a shy, small boy. I keep saying to myself, 'But it is still kitsch!' […] And so is the Supreme Court. Except that there an American pointed out to me that the enormous marble hall would make a perfect bus terminal after a revolution. A second point: the absurd distances in a city with no public transportation. It hinders me in everything I do. I may just have to buy a car. […]

Washington,
November 13, 1938

[*Three days after the* 'Kristallnacht' *pogroms in Germany*]
[…] I am worried about Herbert,[5] about Father, about all those
who again will be hit hard, perhaps even shattered, by the terrible
things happening in Germany that I am reading about in the
newspapers. I am unable even to contemplate the human side of
this new wave of suffering. The political side – and you know that
I really don't want to talk about it because I don't find the other
side as important as you do – is important. Germany could not
have done anything more stupid. I sincerely hope that this will
mean the fall of Chamberlain and that it is not yet too late for
England to regain the support it has lost here. For the time being,
King George is no more than an undesirable alien in a despised
country. That is what Munich achieved here… and it may well be
the most disastrous consequence of Chamberlain's 'deed'.[6] But
enough of politics. […]

Washington,
November 26, 1938

[…]
The princely days of fall are over. Three days ago I was driving in
my roadster through the woods, enjoying the sun and the
warmth, and now it is cold and everything is white with snow.
[…] On Wednesday, in the rain and snow and darkness, I drove
into the city from Capitol Hill. The asphalt was shining from the
reflections of all the lights. And I thought of Amsterdam, cold and
raw, even more stately at dusk than in the gray November light of
day. And I was there, traveling as I have so many times, through

---

5. Herbert Hausmann, German brother-in-law of Max. Forced to give up his
career as a civil servant (*Stadtrat*) in Schweidniz because of his opposition to the
Nazis.

6. Neville Chamberlain, the British Prime Minister who tried to avoid war
between Britain and Germany by negotiating the Munich Agreement with Hitler
in September 1938.

the city to Central Station. Heading home on a Friday or a Saturday. The station swallows you up after the trip through the cold city, and moments later you climb into the welcoming warmth of the train. And then come the mysterious IJ,[7] the polder, and the night sky growing darker and darker until only lights remain. You decide to read your newspaper later and doze off in the safe cozy warmth of the train and with the quiet, happy feeling of going home: Ermelo;[8] and then Amersfoort station. I always enjoy watching the trains to Groningen and Twente. I don't know why but the stretch between Amersfoort and Ermelo always seems very long. But by the time you get to Putten, you are already home. Yes, Putten is already home. Finally, the stationmaster, the telephone call and mother with the car. And then you are really home. Oh, that wonderful wooden house with its warm brown tones![9] [...]

But it's difficult, sometimes very difficult, to know that now again you – and everyone who is trying to keep our circle together – are engulfed in great suffering, with the most far-reaching ramifications. When I think about it, my longing to share it with you is very great indeed, not only because of you but also because of my own loneliness. Because all of this makes one very lonely, the papers are full of it and everyone is expressing horror at what is going on. But it is not *their* world that is caving in. It is not *their* hope that is being trampled underfoot. It is not that they are cold or unfeeling. They are more like a kindly doctor who listens sympathetically to his colleague's recounting of the interesting and terrible disease that killed his wife. They are interested, yes, sometimes moved. But it affects them differently. And that is wholly understandable, maybe even correct. Because we have to go on. And as it was with me in Holland after Munich,[10] and now

---

7. The body of water connecting Amsterdam harbor to the Ijsselmeer, the freshwater lake formed from the Zuiderzee.

8. A village on the east coast of the Ijsselmeer in a wooded area called the Veluwe.

9. The family home, *de Schapendrift* (sheep's trail) built in 1904 from Norwegian pine amid 6 hectares of heather and woods. Destroyed by fire in 1974.

10. Max had been shocked and depressed by the Munich Agreement of September 29 between Hitler, Mussolini, Chamberlain and Daladier in which Hitler was allowed to annex the German-speaking Sudetenland, which had become part of Czechoslovakia after World War I.

would be again, there is no going on. So perhaps it is good that they distance themselves from what is happening, which for me means distancing themselves from me, albeit to a different degree. This said, America may well be the more fruitful, the more obligatory place for me to be at the moment. And maybe it's all right this way: longing for home sometimes but also happy at the thought of that beloved, safe harbor; lonely but not despondent as I was during the days of the Austrian Anschluss and the weeks of the Munich Agreement. And what will it be now? Months? Or will these latest developments drag on for years?

[…]

I want to try to set down what I have established in these first weeks. Mostly for myself but also to give more clarity on both sides of the ocean to the purpose and future direction of my stay here. What follows will abound in assertions that I expect to be read with the qualifiers 'perhaps', 'could be', 'appears to me to be', etc. Don't think that I am daft enough to think that at this point I have even one well-founded opinion. It is just tiring and annoying to keep reiterating that in every sentence.

Now then: the pressure group is the driving force in the state. Politically speaking, the United States consists of factions, not free individuals. Factions with enormous power, equipped with fantastic and unheard-of resources. These pressure groups publicly and behind closed doors campaign, advertise, lobby, twist arms, and corrupt. Every important interest is organized into a powerful faction: the American Legion, Anti-Saloon League, etc., etc. The most important now are the opposing factions: Labor vs Capital, Farmer vs Big Business, Middle Class vs Labor, Labor vs Farmer, etc. Germany […] collapsed under a similar struggle of large, warring factions (class struggle, if you will, but with more than economic factors alone at work). When the struggle becomes so fierce that the social process is violently disturbed and when no one group is strong enough to gain control, the Government must intervene to facilitate adjustment and coordination. To do this, the executive branch needs power – which the warring factions usually try to curtail – but the shock waves produced in the process create a situation that lends itself to a growing concentration of power. The decisive phase in the struggle comes when the Government is able to rally anew a divided people around a common creed: race, world domination, *Blut und Boden* nationalism.[11]

If it succeeds, the Government wins, and the factions disappear, at least from the public eye and as public organizations. [...] The Roosevelt administration at the moment is the all-powerful intervening state. Clashes with all factions, and unbelievable pressure – sometimes corrupt – exerted by the groups themselves, result. The administration [...] frantically rushes to adapt to the new way of thinking about government, which produces more clashes and enormous shifts in the governmental machinery. The upshot at the moment is a tremendous growth in the power of the executive as opposed to the judicial and legislative branches. In fact, all three functions – so sharply separated in the Constitution – are increasingly being carried out by the President and his secretary. [...]

The Roosevelt administration has a social policy but neither the time nor the desire to think about the basic values that determine that policy. It is far too caught up in statistics for that: unemployment, wages and hours, indexes, etc., etc. There is a vague humanism but is that enough to live on? The situation is quite interesting but not at all without danger. As I see it, if war comes, there is barely enough spiritual backbone here to withstand an aggressive fascism. The only solution is to be rooted in Christianity. More important than my conviction of this is the fact that a group of young people at Harvard thinks the same. [...]

So, that is a rough, hastily put together sketch of the image of America that I have formed in my first month here. What to do to improve on this image? I must get to know more. That means working, reading, becoming more familiar with the terminology, seeing people – here in Washington but also at other universities: Harvard, Columbia. Finally, I must see the country [...]. April would be perfect for visiting the South, and then the Midwest –

---

11. 'Blood and soil' was a phrase adopted by Hitler and the Nazis to justify depriving Jews of German citizenship. Originally, it simply meant that people of German descent had the right to live on German soil. The phrase was popularized in 1930 by Walter Darre, Minister of Agriculture for the Third Reich, to establish a link between race and land.

the heart of the country. If I go there in June, I can stay with the parents of one of the students here. That seems to me not unimportant because they know everybody in Kansas, and the Midwest is difficult for a foreigner. Expenses – until August, say – including boat trip and car, would be about $1,000. I find it immensely difficult to say whether all of this – time, money and a few other sentimental things – is worth it. But I am inclined to say yes. I am convinced that I would return from such a trip with an accurate picture of America. And I am also convinced that this is important. But I don't know if it will help me much further in Holland. I am very curious to know how you feel about it. […] With a little luck, I will hear from you around December 15 and then take it from there.

Ermelo,
December 11, 1938

Dear Son,
I may be mistaken, but the trip to the South and the Midwest comes across to me as nothing more than a bit of sightseeing and recreation, certainly not an important part of your education. On top of that are the financial considerations. You estimate the cost of the trip including car at $1,000. That must surely be $1,000 over and above the 2,000-guilder letter of credit that you already have. Because, assuming your equivalency of one dollar to one guilder, such a trip including car – which I am to infer from your letter that you have already bought – plus your keep would be impossible to finance for $1,000. In any case, I think that you should use your inheritance from your grandmother to pay for any expenses that exceed your budget for the 1938–39 academic year. That money was originally intended for a study trip. You still have – after the division of the common account – about 2,000 guilders. I think it is only fair – also to your sisters and Dolph[12] – that you use this money to finance your trip. I think it would also be better for you. You can then determine for yourself whether you have sufficiently weighed the sacrifice in time and money that the trip would entail. I cannot judge the situation from here and you should therefore not take these reservations for anything more that what they are: preliminary considerations.
Very much love,
Father

Washington,
December 4, 1938

[…] Last week I wrote about the 'pluralistic' character of the state, the dramatically conflicting interests that result, and the need to have something to combat the havoc they create. This 'something'

---

12. Eldest brother of Max and father of Dolph Kohnstamm, compiler and editor of this correspondence.

may be centralized power – Hitler, Mussolini in the extreme, Daladier in a milder form[13] – or a common creed – be it Christ or Anti-Christ. And I described, if I remember correctly, a bit of the anti-symbols crusade being carried out by Washington, and the dangers that accompany it.

Since then, something else has become clearer to me. It does not contradict what I wrote last week but may well be, at least in part, the other side of the coin. It is the pragmatism, the resilience and the enthusiasm of the New Deal experiment. There is an ebullience, a feeling that the future is not only worth the gamble but a very good bet. The rebuilding of America! [...] The space that has been created for non-symbolic, pragmatic thinking is inexpressibly refreshing. Of course, there is a large group watching the process from the sidelines in a sort of religious indignation. But it doesn't have very much effect.

Looking back on the recent months in Holland, I have the feeling that we were largely preoccupied by the terrible threat from the east, by the fear of undermining from within and the infiltration of despised and dreaded ideas. We were asking questions such as, How can a democracy exist if there are no commonly held social principles? and Is democracy the rule of the majority? From my vantage point here, I begin to get the idea that while this all may be interesting, it is of little relevance. Because in Holland there is no majority seeking dictatorial power and, however vague, there are rules of the game.

What I did not think about then, because it seemed more a question for the economic experts, was: How can society solve the problem of a just distribution of goods? Economic democracy as necessity, of course, but with the possible exception of some leading social democrats and liberals united in the *'Plan van de Arbeid'*, nobody in Holland gets worked up about the problem. And this is precisely the problem that is now occupying the minds of everybody here, experts or not. And because people believe they can go a long way towards resolving the issue, they are having a lot of fun, whereas we most definitely are not. Here

---

13. Edouard Daladier, premier of France who participated in the Munich Pact with Hitler, Mussolini and Chamberlain.

there is discussion of capitalism together with social equality and social justice – and active striving for it as well. In Holland, the subject of capitalism – at least among respectable people – never comes up, does it? It doesn't come up here either but that is because it is a non-issue.

It sometimes seems as if the most conservative 'New Dealer' would find our Social Democratic Labor Party conservative and backward, while in Holland it isn't even a significant factor. I find it terribly difficult to convey – it all sounds very unimportant and exceedingly superficial. But it comes down to this: [I think] there is a fascinating and positive job to be done in Holland. Nobody has to wait until the country becomes Nazi or is at war to get active. There is work to do… now. Roosevelt successfully fired up a large part of the American people to work at achieving social justice. [Our prime minister] Colijn only sought support for our unthreatened public institutions.

Sometimes I hear the American policy of neutrality defended as follows: 'But can't you see that we are busy building a happier and better society? Do we have to give all that up to help you?' I am not saying that this rationale is reasonable or morally correct, but would not our policy of neutrality have taken on another color in September if Colijn had given us a bit of this enthusiasm, a bit of this youthful vigor? But you have to be radical to do that… which Holland is not and America most definitely is.

Washington,
December 11, 1938

[…]
Quiet days are followed by hours when my emotions run high. Then, the slow permeation of the fabric of American society suddenly picks up speed, bringing great discoveries – or great disappointments. Today I want to replace the summary news reports of my recent letters with a report from the heart. […]

America, and more America. I believe that each day brings me a step closer to understanding its social, political and cultural character. I particularly believe that I can see the directions in which I will be able to proceed. And I have the feeling that it is important to complete this project to the extent that it is possible. I certainly do not believe that setting out with no preparation and having to make the best of a bad job has been the most appropriate approach. But on the other hand, as an experiment, it has been unusually interesting, and the few months I could have saved do not weigh up against my personal gain, which is a direct result of the difficulties encountered. The purpose of the trip to America was not just America but also the chance to be on one's own, to stand on one's own two feet. And it's working, apart from the deplorably weak and deformed foot that is the financial one. Ernst[14] says – and I think I will follow his advice – that if need be, I should not hesitate to swindle Father out of even more money than I have done already.

It must sound foolish when a youngster like me writes that he is worried about the United States of America. But there is something here – experimenting, building for the future, courage, spunk, willingness to bear burdens and a joy in living – all the ingredients for golden opportunity – and there is sometimes a childish ignorance of the wickedness of the world. And you wonder how much of this will become chilled, twisted and broken in the confrontation with the evil of Nazism. Do not let the newspaper reports about Germany and the great sense of outrage that prevails here deceive you. Very few people truly understand the situation. America is so young and absorbed in its own hemisphere that it simply cannot understand how old and angry Europe is. No, the gulf between Europe and America is deep and wide. And more than that: throwing up a temporary bridge so that they can come help us out of our misery would, I think, be a terrible injustice. America must remain neutral until it grows up enough to understand its reasons for going to war. [...] The consequences of a war for America and for the world would be far worse, it seems to me, if the USA were to become involved because it would mean the loss of its beliefs and ideals.

[...]

---

14. Ernst van der Beugel, close friend of Max. In later life, assistant secretary of foreign affairs and CEO of KLM Royal Dutch Airlines.

But here in America – so far from gloom and despair – I see that the tragedy of Europe renders our lives not only more angst-ridden and less joyful but richer and deeper as well. We are living at another level. Not more happily... and not more realistically, because it is only according to the European reality. But I don't think it would be easy, or give more value to life, to exchange Europe for America. [...] Until now, I have found very little to match the deep solidarity among people that is a certitude in Holland.

Ermelo,
December 21, 1938

Dear Son!
And now America! And your explications of it. Most of what you say does not surprise me at all. My experiences with virtually all Americans I have met are similar to yours. But what has become much clearer to me, especially in your most recent letter – although I had naturally expected it – is the pressure that post-1931 Europe has exerted not only on our older generation but also on your generation. What you are now experiencing in America as something completely new is the self-evident joy and certitude of life that until my 55th year seemed so obvious to me that I could not have thought otherwise (and which was also apparent – despite the hardship caused by the Depression – in the expectations of the future in the socialist working class; I believe it was apparent as well, although different, in the Christian segment of our nation). I wrote about this in the final chapters of *De Heilige*,[15] but in such a way that I can now only look upon it as having been written long, long ago.

Meanwhile, it is for exactly that reason that I cannot agree with your conclusions regarding the legitimacy – yes, the call to duty – of American isolationism and the let-Europe-fend-for-itself attitude.

---

15. *De Heilige* (The Holy), the title of the last volume of Philip Kohnstamm's trilogy *Schepper en Schepping* (Creator and Creation), published in 1931.

You forget, it occurs to me, that the upheaval in Europe is for a large part the fault of America! Specifically, its intervention in the World War and its total failure to convert the then loudly proclaimed slogans of democracy and the League of Nations into reality. Had America not intervened in the World War, it would have been a draw, thereby creating a situation that would have come closer to a real peace than Versailles did. It would have included keeping intact the traditional German army and the Hohenzollern dynasty (which we now view as a far less dangerous period than the current one). The world would have probably been spared the monumental inferiority complex and grave collective psychosis of Germany today.

Instead, America participated… and pulled out at the exact moment when real, adult statesmanship was needed, namely at the armistice when Wilson's program was being implemented. This is not cheap wisdom in hindsight, twenty years down the line. On November 12, 1918, when the conditions of the armistice were published, I saw it and said so in public.

What one could not see then – at least as far as I know, no one saw it, least of all the economists – was the tremendous revolution in manufacturing conditions as a result of the wartime and post-wartime modernization of companies. And here we arrive at the point where you apparently – and, in my opinion, correctly – feel yourself to be most attracted by the new and young America with its limitless opportunities. Because you are witnessing, from relatively nearby, something of the transition from capitalistic to socialistic production methods, i.e., from production guided by price and cost levels to production based on need. Since this has apparently become the focal point of your stay in America, it is a pity that you do not have more knowledge of economic theory. That certainly would have been a very good preparation. But I suspect you are already busy learning more about it there. What continues to strike me from the scant and unsystematic newspaper reports I have seen on the subject is that the New Deal approaches everything from the money side and not from the product or supply side as in Russia and Germany. I am still of the impression that the latter, in their five- and four-year-plan economies, dare to be more radical and therefore have more chance of success, even if it is at the expense of all non-material things, that is to say, of what truly matters. I get the idea from your letters, however, that your Washington and New York environment causes you to underestimate the opposing forces [in the US] (and maybe even some of the pragmatically correct objections to New Deal policies). Because it is really quite remarkable how diametrically opposed your 'impressions of America' are to those which Uncle Guus formed during his summer there.[16] His trip was shorter, but he had intense contacts with a number of people who are also very typically American. Everything that attracts you, he found terribly wrong and, what is more, terribly stupid and short-sighted. So if you want to see both sides of the picture, you should definitely try to acquaint yourself as well with the views of Wall Street and Business. Perhaps the introductions from Van der Beugel will be sufficient to do that.[17] He ought to be able to provide introductions to Wall Street financiers. Their views are surely very different from those of industry. From the social psychological point of view, I think it is very important to hear directly what people have to say, and particularly how the workers in industry themselves view their position and future prospects in America.

What you wrote about the big, organized pressure groups and their power interested me very much. I already knew a bit about them from reading several books about congressional lobbies. Nonetheless, I think that you underestimate the similarity in this respect with Europe (France, for example), even in our own country, where everything of course happens on a much smaller scale. That difference in scale, which may be more than just a difference in mentality, also plays a big role in what you called the 'conservatism of Holland' in your second-to-last letter. You know, of course, that I was never an admirer of Colijn's liberal economy. But the things that can be achieved in the United States with a population 15 times larger and a surface area some 300 times greater, with its correspondingly vast amounts of mineral

---

16. J.B.A. Kessler, younger brother of Max's mother and uncle of Max. CEO of Royal Dutch/Shell Group. Son of J.B.A. Kessler senior, the co-founder of Royal Dutch Petroleum Company.
17. Banker in Amsterdam and father of Ernst van der Beugel.

resources and raw materials (don't forget that!), are just radically different than in Holland. Probably this has something to do with what you were saying in your last letter about the deep and more personal relationships in Holland. That is the other side of the coin. Is it not very much a question of quantity (mass) and quality? For many years now there has been no doubt in my mind that, if the transition from individual output to collective output is to succeed without the complete depersonalization of man (as in the totalitarian states), America will have to point the way. But I also see, prompted by my fairly intimate knowledge of American education, the serious danger of sacrificing quality to quantity.

Well, I have not written such a long letter without dictation in years. The Christmas holiday atmosphere and the holiday itself, which already promises not to be too busy, presented the opportunity. And thus it is fitting, even though it may not reach you until 1939, to wish you a Merry Christmas and a Happy New Year – your first in a foreign land. May it be a rich and rewarding year for you.
Father

Northampton,
December 27, 1938

Dearest Mother,
First, a few business matters: if you want a letter to reach me quickly, please indicate the name of the boat. That saves about a week. Letters often take ridiculously long to get here – two weeks or more. [...]

Floor wrote to me about skiing plans.[18] Brrr! And that atop the extreme cold spell that you have already had! Has there been any ice-skating? I am afraid that the cold was very bad for Father. I so hope that his Christmas vacation is somewhat of a real vacation. His letter was waiting for me here in Northampton. Wonderful… I will return to that later. It is kind of him to have found the time to give all this advice from such a distance! [...]

---

18. Floor Ingen Housz, friend of Max who later married his sister Uus.

At the moment, the situation here is as follows: America has really got hold of me. I am beginning to feel at home and the country's youthfulness and resilience are starting to have a strong and seductive effect on me. It is so very difficult to describe. But Europe is sometimes unbelievably far away. Not even that, it simply doesn't exist. Germany and Italy are hated here, but without depth or bitterness. Totally different from our intense dislike. No, America is living in great isolation and I don't think that at such a distance it can be otherwise. And you really have no idea how fascinating America itself is. The optimism, the enthusiasm and the belief in its own cause! [...] Dangers lurk on all sides: racial hatred, violence, class struggle, group egotism. But that does not weigh up against the disarming naivety and the goodwill. It doesn't go deep, no, but it is so unbelievably refreshing after Europe. [...]

There is of course the other side: the Negro question, very strong anti-Semitism. And the ever-burgeoning wealth. Will there never be room for any other ideal than 'bigger and better'? In a couple of years, we will be traveling from New York to San Francisco for $5. An invention that may be as revolutionary as the automobile. Will it be a force for the better or for the worse? Or will there be groups capable of keeping the country in a state of perpetual distress? That will bring revolution. It almost happened in 1932 and 1933. And it can definitely happen again. But it needn't. [...]

Hopkins, the radical, the red, the trust buster and business hater from whom you would have expected, at the most, a vague materialistic humanism, announced the day after he was sworn in on the Bible as Secretary of Commerce – and the Bible was a present from Mr. and Mrs. Roosevelt – 'The story of Christmas is the hope of mankind.'

I think that you and Father would really enjoy a trip here. Father would be better able than I to see the good things and find value where I only see shallowness. No, as long as America exists, there is hope. [...]

I have given a great deal of thought to Father's letter, but I still believe that I must proceed with my plan. Johnson was most helpful to me in New York.[19] He supported my plan and will expand it further, providing me with introductions everywhere. Terribly nice. He spoke exceptionally well of Father. […]

I am wholly in agreement with Father's financial arrangements, but I suspect that $1,000–1,500 will be sufficient. I live very modestly here, although you may not believe that. If Father has no more reservations, I will stay here through June, and probably both the summer months as well. But please let me know if you don't agree or feel uncomfortable with my decision. If an opportunity for Herbert arises, I will hand over my letter of credit, introductions and car to him tomorrow. And that is no idle boast.

The [Kotschnig] children here defy description. I say that in all seriousness. America's public enemy no.1: progressive education. You can't even imagine the bedlam, tyranny and guerrilla warfare. Like timid, fearful shadows, adults maneuver around the house, trying to stay out of the way of the omnipotent child despots holding court. Children of three monopolize the radio; at five they take over the telephone, wisecracking to their friends, and at seven or eight, they commandeer the car. Father has to walk – or buy a second car. Yelling and fighting, slamming doors or leaving them open, they rampage through the house like a herd of elephants. They usually carry guns and you can be grateful if they load them with rubber darts because these are less painful than lead pellets. You can also consider yourself lucky if you know how to sit on the floor, because the chairs are theirs. As are the newspapers, books, and magazines. Sometimes a juicy detective keeps them quiet for a few minutes or a trip to the movies brings relief.

I haven't yet discovered which is best for parents: a war between the children or a dictatorial pact. In the first instance, the youngest offspring are mentally and physically demolished, just like the house. But if you are very smart, you can act as a kind of 'balancing power' to give yourself a semblance of authority. In the

---

19. F. Ernest Johnson, executive secretary of the Department of Research and Education of the Federal Council of the Churches of Christ in America (New York), now called the National Council of Churches of Christ in the USA.

second instance, your children grow up nicely but you yourself become the poor victim of their capriciousness. But it has to be said, I have seen children who sometimes show mercy and throw some crumbs to their parents or allow them to watch Shirley Temple when they go off to see their 'fellow gangsters' at the movies.

Sometimes, in the midst of this intoxication of ever-changing impressions, people, cities, and landscapes, moments of stillness suddenly emerge. Listening to music, sitting in a church or gazing up at a skyscraper in New York. New York, where the harbor lies and the wide ocean begins, the boundary but also the lifeline to Holland… to all that I cherish: Ermelo, land of my youth where every tree, every sound, every cloud was familiar to me. Where is life going to take me? The life that for many is so unutterably hard now. Will there be a job for me close to home, close to you? Will there be a job and a future at all in Europe? Or only death, war and ruin. Nobody knows. […]

P.S. It galls me that I have to use a German boat to send this letter but all the others are out cruising!

Northampton,
December 30, 1938

[…]
The behavior of the Kotschnig children really does defy all description. Any attempt to carry on a conversation at the dinner table is totally impossible. And not only during dinner but after dinner as well – until they finally go to bed at 9 or 10 p.m. They are not nasty or bad children, just casualties of a complete lack of guidance. For the first time in my life I have found myself in the position of having to restrain myself at least every five minutes from giving one of the three a good thrashing – mostly the two older children; the youngest is a fairly timid boy (no small wonder). The noise, the slovenliness and the rudeness – or shall we say unmannerliness – spoil almost every gathering. The first day you think it's funny but then it's over. To make matters worse, there is a new radio.

Oh well, I am getting better at dealing with this sort of thing. […] Walter and his wife have been very friendly. And, I must not forget, they are very loving towards each other. They carry their cross – the children – without complaint. […]

The problem has its interesting aspects. The daughter (aged 12 or 13) can look adorable but your hair stands on end when you see what she reads (detectives and magazines) and what she watches (two or three movies a week). Of course, it is very difficult for any set of parents to buck this American trend. But you know as well as I do what the dangers are in the absence of an enormous amount of care and devotion. There is a precocity that makes your heart stand still. And it fits perfectly with what I have seen in several other families with other children: a disillusionment, a disenchantment with all the fun and games. […] On the other hand, the exact opposite – the disarming openness, the naivety – is still there as well.

There is also an admirable sense of duty. An incredible stoicism to take things as they come without complaint. For example, there is a girl from Kansas in my house in Washington. Unattractive, an appallingly loud voice, but invincible in her industry and optimism. Hard working, very hard working. She spent her two-week vacation at Christmas working in a shop in Washington. I assure you that she did not do that for her own pleasure. And that she was longing to be home with her beloved father, mother, brothers and sisters. But you never heard a word of complaint. Missing, of course, are the charms that culture and a 'leisure class' upbringing afford one. But it is very healthy. That is the other side.

This exceptional side was also apparent to me at a meeting I attended in a nearby country village: a sort of church council consisting of Walter Kotschnig, the minister, three farmers (without any sign of our usual farming attire) and two women. Everyone was wonderfully open-minded, well informed, interested. The purpose of the meeting was to determine whether the congregation would be able to adopt a refugee family. You would have enjoyed it!

Nonetheless, it is good that I continue to see clearly the shadow side of things now and then lest I become too enamored of this unspoiled and promising land.

Floor Ingen Housz has written me a very somber and bitter letter. Yes, that is Holland; that is Europe. Although there is still that other side of Holland that makes you forget all the misery. I think of so many weekends in Ermelo. Will that not still be possible this year? Don't think that Floor's letter only puts me off; it also makes me long for the difficult but intellectually demanding life that a job in Holland offers. I don't think America can entice me to stay if I am able to find work to do in Holland. The choice would be harder, however, if there were to be no place for me in Holland. But these are distant and idle reflections.

As I write, I see that it has become December 31. One more day and 1939 begins. What will it hold for me? Whether my plans meet with success, whether my trip is fruitful or no more than a bit of sightseeing, as Father fears, remains to be seen. I will try to keep my eyes and ears wide open and approach each day with an open mind. And then will come a day in the new year, a distant day but not so distant that it does not time and time again intrude upon my thoughts, when I will be home again!

Washington,
January 8, 1939

[…]
Saturday I received your and father's letter of December 21. (Our letters to each other certainly take their time, don't they!) The letter from you, Father, made me very happy. Not only because of your caring and concern but also because of a kind of son's pride in the way you were able to appraise a country you have never even seen, hitting one nail on the head after another. I think you would both really benefit from a taking a trip to America at some point. […] I think it would be very good for you both.

I have already written to you about my plans; you will see that they entail more traveling than you think advisable. I am prepared to stop instantly if things become too superficial or hurried. […] In one respect, I have drastically altered my comings and goings. On Walter's advice, I have chosen a more specific topic to study –

labor – and I am reading less and contacting more people. It may sound silly but to be able to say I am studying this or that makes things much easier. [...]

I held an after-dinner speech for a YMCA group last Saturday on the subject of Holland and America. It really went very nicely. If I take a quieter look around me now, after those first stormy months, I increasingly feel my future is not here – for a whole complex of reasons, in which solidarity with Holland plays an appreciably bigger role than my sense of duty. No, if there are opportunities for me in Holland, if there is something useful for me to do, I think now that a decision would not be very difficult to make. A not unimportant factor is the feeling that your innermost self would not be able to find employment here. Despite the goodwill and Roosevelt's magnificent message to Congress,[20] you miss profundity. At the same time, I believe that we Dutch should come here often in search of new optimism, courage and vigor.

Today I attended a service in the Howard University chapel. A beautiful service but a sermon of exceptional flabbiness. At first I had the feeling that this Negro group, with all of its trials and tribulations, could provide evangelism with the stimulus it so often lacks here. But the sermon, which started out well, skidded sideways and ended up with the admonition to 'seek the happiness of St Francis and Schweitzer'. Now, in my view, this is not the problem. America's problem is this: enormous wealth is within everyone's reach but only if everyone understands that securing it is not life's primary task. [...]

The weather here is beautiful beyond description. Every day is sunny and warm. Usually the best weather is at the end of April. Today I went for a drive in my roadster, took a walk with Jane[21]

---

20. Roosevelt's Annual Message to the Congress of January 4, 1939, from which comes the famous passage:

> 'There comes a time in the affairs of men when they must prepare to defend, not their homes alone, but the tenets of faith and humanity on which their churches, their governments and their civilization are founded. The defense of religion, of democracy and of good faith among nations is all the same fight.'

21. Jane Hillebrand, a student at the George Washington University in Washington DC, became a close friend of Max.

and slept in the sun at 4:00 in the afternoon. Is that not enough to entice you to come for a visit?

Very, very much love and an embrace,

Your Max

Ermelo,
Jan. 21, 1939

Dear Son! Your letter of January 8 arrived this morning. The rare occasion of an unoccupied Saturday afternoon affords me the opportunity to respond to this letter as well as to your previous ones.

I am convinced of what you say about the desirability – with an eye to the American mentality – of keeping deliberations brief. One gets the same impression of Americans when they come here. In itself, it is a shortcoming, of course: a typical *multa, non multum.*[22] A bit similar to the use of 'discussion groups' to solve difficult problems rather than allowing a few people to examine them quietly and in depth, as they used to do in New England. It is a search for solutions in the horizontal. I recall animated conversations on the subject with Abel Gregg from YMCA headquarters in New York.

Walter Kotschnig's advice to put a label on your study intentions seems to me very wise. Not only for others but also for yourself. You did not, however, say whether you have incorporated that advice into your plan as yet, or what you are going to do after Washington. Let us know as soon as possible.

By the way, a quick note about the financial side of things: As you requested, I let the money transfers continue through December 28, which means an additional 330 guilders to your account. Excluding the 1,337 guilders for the trip, travel money, and letter of credit withdrawal (was that the car?), this comes to roughly 2,300 guilders over 1938. I am now stopping the money transfers. We will figure out your 1939 expenses later. [...]

I am delighted to see that Roosevelt's address to Congress also

---

22. 'Intense but not for long'.

had such an important effect from nearby. Can you supply me with the official text? Here we only received short (translated!) summaries. I would like to have it in its entirety for an article I have to write in early March on *Personalism and the World Situation* for an American journal.[23]

I could not have guessed that there is as much anti-English sentiment in America as you describe. Do you think that it will continue, even if, say, Chamberlain were to make room for Eden? If so, that would be very serious indeed, because as far as I can see a united Anglo-Saxon front is about all that stands between our times and worldwide spiritual chaos.

Despite Schacht's resignation last night,[24] I don't for a minute believe there will be an economic or financial collapse of this reign of terror. It is constructed much too well for that, especially in its approach to economic output. That is the real strength of National Socialism, precisely because it is socialism and actually stolen from Russia. As for the need to find raw materials, that is not a spiritual but a technical problem and they will certainly be able to solve it. But of course the big question remains of whether everything that makes life worth living as a human being will not be sacrificed in the process.

I also understand very well what you, in this connection, are saying about the appeal of the American way of life, its joyfulness and hope for the future. But what you also say about the danger of the securing of wealth becoming the primary task in life, that is indeed the powerful force that seems to have enabled Hitler in just a few short years to deliver a mortal blow to the *Geist des Volkes der Dichter und Denker*.[25] "What do Germans care if they no longer have a free press when they can ride in a cheap Volkswagen instead?" Indeed, if this materialistic mentality were also to move

---

23. *The Personalist: a quarterly journal of philosophy, religion and literature.* Philip Kohnstamm's article appeared in the fall issue of 1939.

24. Hjalmar Schacht, President of the Central Bank of the Third Reich and Minister of Economic Affairs. Resigned from the ministry in 1937 and from the Central Bank in January 1939. Was sent to a concentration camp by the Nazis after the failed attempt on Hitler's life in 1944. Cleared by the war crimes tribunal at Nurnberg in 1946.

25. 'The spirit of the people of poets and philosophers'.

America and cause it to drift away from the Biblical anchoring of its drive for improvement, then that excellent servant of mankind would become its devilish master. Because what other source is there for resistance? For now, we will simply have to assume that Yahweh will prove to be more powerful than Baal in the 20th century as well. And that out of this world crisis will emerge the possibility of a deeper, more secure spiritual existence, accessible to everyone, and not the end of spiritual life altogether.

It is exactly in this respect that I found Roosevelt's address, binding belief, democracy, and international good faith, so marvelous. How the Barthians of ten years ago would have come down on that had not Barth himself changed course and come to the same conclusion.[26] Who knows, maybe the sufferings of our time are just labor pains. [...]

Finally, one more thing! Aunt Go[27] is sending me today a noteworthy news item about an experiment to reduce unemployment on a vast scale in Minneapolis, Minnesota. After a visit to Russia, a Wesleyan minister called Dr. Mecklenburg some fifteen months ago succeeded in setting up an organization of unemployment cooperatives, whereby thousands are now gainfully employed. (Address: Secretary Earl Lenth, headquarters, Vocational High School, Fourth Avenue and 11th Street, Minneapolis.) It seems much too good to be true. But if it is true, it alone is worth a trip to Minneapolis. Have you heard of it? In any case, it wouldn't take much effort to write them or find out about it in some other way

Well, so much for today,
Father

---

26. Karl Barth (1886-1968), pre-eminent Swiss Protestant theologian, professor at the University of Basel after being dismissed as professor in Bonn because of his refusal to take the oath of allegiance to Hitler.
27. Younger sister of Max's mother.

Washington,
January 15, 1939

[…] Sometimes I think that I am learning at least as much about myself here as about America. My only serious worry is the international situation. Even the reports in a newspaper as reliable as the *New York Times* are ominous for Holland. And sometimes I am beset by the appalling angst that our Dutch Government will gradually give in to German demands. But maybe this is a failure on my part to have faith in one's own people. War would be terrible but a Germanized Holland far worse. It is difficult sometimes to cope with all of this alone. Jane helps me a little now and then.

Washington,
January 24, 1939

[…] It occurs to me, from this vantage point, that the Colijn Government is totally lacking in leadership, without the least bit of hankering for justice. Despite my thousands of complaints about America, it is so much more alive here. Where has that feeling gone to in Holland? My friends Piet and Wibo have both written me extremely somber letters in this respect. Our own group, with the exception of Father, seems to me to be so at fault, so lulled into a sense of false security.

[…] The knowledge I am acquiring here I consider mainly journalistic – in the best sense of the word. First, it is amazingly interesting and secondly, I believe, very broadening. It gives me better insight into the social forces at play, releases me from a big burden – that of post-Munich hopelessness – and fires me up with a good dose of dissatisfaction with the existing social order. Which, for now, I put on the positive side of the ledger.

[Max then asks himself in this letter whether he should perhaps become a journalist or go into politics in Holland, and whether he should not look for a job in America, at a university or working as a journalist for the Dutch national daily newspaper NRC.*]*

The reason that I want to stay here until May or even June is that I still feel I am learning a lot and need to sharpen and strengthen my impressions. [...] In the unlikely event that I remain solvent, I may stay even longer, using the final months for a vacation trip. I have heard so much about California.

I have seen thousands of people in scores of government offices, at Howard University, the CIO, AFL, Farm Union, etc. The highlight was an interview with Sir Wilmott Lewis of the London *Times*, thanks to an introduction by Mr. van der Beugel. It was rich and unforgettable. And today I had a very interesting lunch with Francis Miller, one of the most charming men I have ever met. His Southern accent is sublime.

February 11, 1939

[…]

Monday, January 30, I spent in Richmond, Virginia, and from Tuesday to Friday, February 10, at Duke University in Durham, North Carolina and the University of North Carolina in Chapel Hill. Yesterday, I visited a Farm Security Administration Homestead Settlement. And tonight, a night turned suddenly cold and stormy, I am staying in a silent, deserted hotel 90 miles north of Charleston, South Carolina. Tomorrow, or the next day if the distance is too great, I hope to be in Atlanta, Georgia – the metropolis of the South.

I left Washington on a wet and cheerless day… the first such day in weeks. The Potomac River, the road, the light and the land were all gray. And I was also a little bit sad. Because even though Jane was the only real tie I had with Washington, I nonetheless am the sort who makes decisions easily but carries them out with difficulty. America stretched endlessly ahead of me and there was not a familiar face to be found anywhere among the millions. […]

The problem these past two weeks has been the South. Already in Richmond I felt as if I were in another country. The weather had cleared, turning sunny and warm, and Professor Rolvix Harland took me to view the state capital from a hill above the city. People were sitting on benches in the sun, strolling on the street, speaking with that slow, melodious drawl. It reminded me more of France and southern Europe than of America. The hospitality, the pleasant, leisurely tempo and unfamiliar dialect, the rolling wooded landscape and the warmth, sun and torrential rains. There is more of a sense of really living, perhaps, than in the North. But that is only the one side: charming, friendly and for me enchanting – as I am always enchanted by the sun wherever I am.

The other side came soon enough. That evening the topic of conversation turned to the plight of the Negro. The abject misery of these subjugated people, the impossibility of inviting a colleague from the Negro university to your home, the Negro maid who is not allowed to sleep under the same roof as her white employer. And then there is the angst, the half-heartedness, the self-reproach of the whites. Later, when I was in Durham, I talked to a Negro editor. He was genial, witty, and more optimistic about the situation than most of the people at Howard. And that made it all the more poignant when he recounted without a trace of bitterness the dangerous situation he had been in when he dined with two ultra-left white politicians. It was not the fact that they were ultra-left but that they were white and he was at the same table with them. The situation was dangerous, he said, 'but it was the most beautiful day of my life. I really felt like a human being'.

The University of North Carolina is a very liberal university. I met boys who talked about their attempts to tear down the barriers. Some were full of courage and enthusiasm, others bitter. Professors sometimes made jokes about the situation, others were exhausted and broken, too often hurt by the taunting irrationality and now hardened. [...] There was the vehement protest of Professor Ericson, but there were also the forty students who had participated in the last – fortunately unsuccessful – lynching. There were the Negro women in the Chesterfield tobacco plant, singing the same spirituals that were sung in the days of slavery, only they were not as well cared for and perhaps even more wretchedly housed. [...] Then there was the University of Tobacco Workers, an AFL affiliate, but extremely well organized. And unremittingly over all of it, the problem of the South: poverty and the farm question.

The first evening I drove through the warm, moonlit night from Durham to Chapel Hill. It was quiet and the darkness cloaked the indescribable misery that daylight had made manifest to me. Houses whose existence I would never have imagined in a rural community: filthy, decrepit, one or two rooms, children in rags. And the land: ripped apart, washed away, untended, and barren. The woods a wasteland, sometimes washed over by the reddish brown waters of a creek. The reckless squandering and abuse of the land made me almost sick that first day. And it is all the more unfathomable if you then drive through the warm, moist night, perfumed even now with the overwhelming scent of spring, into a small, silent village and from the window of your quiet, clean hotel room gaze out over the peaceful campus. [...]

The Southerner, without exception, takes it easy. He enjoys life, and the Yankee does not. But that does not alter the fact of infant mortality, misery, malnutrition and disease. There are states here that spend only one-twentieth of the money spent by the North on education. And that amount has to fund two systems of education: colored and white. ...In the past two days I have visited two of the Farm Security Administration settlements, which are a huge attempt to solve the farm problem in a revolutionary way through a combination of education and cheap long-term loans [...] That is, until the Agricultural Adjustment Administration comes along and retires the land because of overproduction.

There is so much to relate about university life. I stayed in a fraternity and had every opportunity to observe campus life in detail. The students are very young and the educational system is much like our secondary schools. Nonetheless, the system is reaching twice as many people this way. And your criticism, Father, of the unscientific approach, shallowness, total absence of style and whatever else of the American educational system is suddenly muted when you discover after a 15-minute conversation with a family on a small farm – who with the help of Washington are just able to keep their heads above water – that the son is working his way through college or that the wife has a B.A.

[...]

The South is like quicksand. Once you step into it, it is very difficult to get out again. The problem is that my mail is piling up in Chattanooga, where according to my itinerary, I was supposed to have been a week ago. I am really going to have to hunt to track it down. And any urgent messages should have been forwarded through Washington.

On Monday, with the top down on my roadster, I left Atlanta. The drive through the surrounding mill towns was a bit sinister but no worse than expected. Mill town company-owned houses, company-owned stores, company-owned streets. Sometimes on Saturdays, an empty pay envelope because the rent for the store or the house is deducted and there is nothing left. Twelve dollars: the American standard of starving. Or you get paid in company-issued coupons instead of cash. Here and there the Labor Union has made inroads. But it is difficult. Management plays the Negro off against the white. Divide and conquer. The Klan is riding again. Are they assisting the law? But who is the law? Maybe the sheriff is feeling witty and tells you he will inform your wife if you are lynched. If this is the law, you are better off looking after your own safety.

Attendance at the CIO meeting in Douglasville, Georgia, consisted of two organizers, eighteen workers, and two who had been fired because of union activity (a flagrant flouting of the law, but then Washington is too far away to notice). There were also two rifles, one handgun, one portrait of Jesus in Gethsemane and one of Roosevelt. The curtains were drawn and for all the money in the world I wouldn't have wanted to get on the wrong side of the man who was guarding the door. The meeting was opened with a prayer. But the minister is paid by the mill and preaches every Sunday about the Mark of the Beast and the CIO. How long will these people be able to separate their Church from the Bible?

Fortunately, there is also the other South. The garden village of West Point, Georgia, for example: lush and green, roomy houses, well-tended gardens, a few cows and chickens. Just having one Coca-Cola there was enough to discover that life here is good. A weekly wage runs $12–35 and you can rent a house for $1 per room per month or half the usual price of $2. In other places a farmer can starve to death as easily as a laborer. With a farmer's share of only two-thirds of the crop, at current prices, there is little left to live on.

One-third of Georgia's inhabitants are Negro. Twelve percent of hospital beds are set aside for Negroes. Mortality is twice that of whites. Sixty-five percent of all tuberculosis cases are in the Negro population. But in West Point, I saw a black university settlement and a black Federal Housing Administration: well-kept homes, gardens, children playing and a fine Negro manager, full of hope for the future. […] *Up from Slavery*, the title of the famous book by Booker T. Washington, founder of Tuskegee Institute, sometimes seems like wishful thinking. But that is much too somber. You should not forget that Mrs. Eleazar, the wife of the secretary of the Interracial Commission in Atlanta, was not allowed to read *Uncle Tom's Cabin* as a young girl. And then consider Dr. Raper's (also from the Interracial Commission) class at Agnes Scott College [in Decatur, Georgia]: all girls from good Christian Southern families. When I asked them if they didn't think they were treating the Negroes in precisely the same way as the Germans did the Jews, their response was a sheepish 'Yes.' No excuse, nothing. Nor were they indignant over my question, only saying, 'It takes a long, long time to do away with prejudice. We have such a long, long way to go, you know?'

[…]

Tuskegee lies in the middle of bitterly impoverished farmland, Alabama's black belt, with a population that is more than 50% Negro. It is the site of one of America's oldest and most famous Negro institutes, consisting of a teacher's college, handicraft school, high school, experimental grammar school, junior college and, recently, a four-year college. Tuskegee is a village, and the institute itself, situated a few miles off the road, is also a village. Gloriously green, well tended, fragrant with flowers on a spring afternoon. […] I had a short visit with the president, drew up a sort of agenda for the duration of my stay and then installed myself in the very tidy guesthouse, wholly run by the students, who take care of the rooms and prepare and serve the meals. The only other guests were Mr. and Mrs. Pyle. He is a columnist for the Scripps-Howard newspapers, a New Deal syndicate. Nice people, recently returned from South America and as deeply stirred by the US South as I. Several horrifying and hard-to-believe stories about maltreatment and starvation in the Mississippi Delta.

After dinner I went with the Pyles and several people from Tuskegee to watch basketball in the new gymnasium. Basketball is a highly refined version of our *korfbal*, very exciting to watch and one of the three national college sports. The basketball trainer, together with the football trainer, is usually the best-paid member of the staff. First, we watched a girls' game. Negro girls move with exceptional grace and no less so during the speed of sport, almost never forced. They generally have lean, powerfully built bodies, more robust than the rather limp figures of Southern white girls. There is an immense difference, by the way, between Southern white girls and their Northern counterparts. They are more petite, much better looking and better groomed. But a little too pretty, too doll-like (and darn fast, I am afraid). The girls' game was followed by one for boys under the age of seven. You should have seen it: Negro kids are so incredibly comic to watch!

Afterwards, we strolled home through the moist, sweet-scented spring night. Windows shone in every building. Boys and girls, arm in arm in the good American fashion, sauntering over the campus. A whisper of wind in the live oaks... and crickets. Yes, the South can be quite a 'garden spot'. [...]

I visited the Federal Land Use Project the next afternoon. Eleven thousand acres, abused for so long that even subsistence living had become an impossibility. The federal government bought the land, moved the families out – some to the nearby settlement, others to shacks and holes in the ground – and is now attempting to return the little topsoil that has not washed away to its natural wooded state. Ten families currently inhabit the land, spread out over the project, in nice new homes. After my visit, I spoke with Manager Robers in his office. He told me it was a Negro project, and Tuskegee hoped in time to turn it into a soil conservation research station for agriculture students. Robers is a

by Ernie Pyle

is tasteful, indeed, and easy to look at.

The old massive architecture of the South is passe. Hardly ever do you see a new house going up that is big and square and buttressed by those immense, two-storied white pillars out front. That's Mammy-stuff now.

The houses of today are a story and a half, and they keep dropping down at each end into lower-roofed sun rooms and garages. It gives a rambling person-ality which I like in a house. The South's new archi-tecture is swell.

* * *

Impressions of a Dutchman

WHEN we were at Tuskegee Institute, we met a young man from Holland who is over here on a fellowship, making a study of industrial and labor conditions.

He has spent a couple of months in Washington, and is now swinging through the South in a second-hand roadster he bought in the Capital.

His name is Max Kohnstamm. He speaks excellent English, and in three months has achieved one of the most complete grasps of America I have ever seen in a foreigner. But from our conversations, I believe he will return to Holland with two impressions which stand out above all the others. They are:

1.—That he can't understand why the South, with its warmth and rains and fertile soil, should be drab and bleak-looking, instead of an immense tropical gar-den-spot.

2.—That Sir Wilmott Lewis, the brilliant Washing-ton correspondent for the London Times, is the only person he has met in America who doesn't have a pri-vate secretary.

I couldn't clear up either of these impressions for him. The first one would take too long. And, as for the second, Sir Wilmott has been in America so long that I'll bet he, too, has a secretary hidden behind the screen somewhere.

fine man, a very dark-skinned Negro, young and hopeful. Still, the question needs to be asked: is it possible through education to achieve something within the limits of the existing landowner system? No matter how well-educated, can a tenant who has not got a penny, has never had a penny, who has to borrow money to buy fertilizer, is always in debt, and is never sure of a second winter on the same land, ever achieve anything? On the other hand, the settlements prove that sudden major changes in land use, housing conditions, etc., do not work, either economically or from a purely humanitarian standpoint. Reform must be done gradually and with great patience.

Next, I had a meeting with the extension agent, responsible for the house-to-house farm education of Negroes in Macon County. The extension service is purely educational and does not give subsidies or issue loans. Mr. Turner made a deep impression on me. He was not bitter – I have yet to meet a really bitter Negro – but down and out. His kind, tired face never smiled. Occasionally he would laugh but it was the laugh of someone in great pain… registering the full spectrum of suffering: poverty, hunger, sickness, hatred, lack of education, a land laid waste, a people exploited. And then to think that he had been working for twenty years to change things but had never really been able to help. He said, 'Jim Crow, who is my race, whom I love, is starving to death. He is dying after a life of drudgery and without ever having known anything but misery. Oh well, maybe my children will be able to do something for their children.'

I walked home in the rain. Seated at the table was an African missionary, now a US citizen but who had only been in America for eighteen months, trying to drum up interest in Africa. A quiet, serious, pious man. But if you have had a day as I had just had, your hair stands on end if you then have to hear that alcohol is the cause of all the misery here. And that increasing wages – to more than $12 a week – will not help because then everything will become too expensive. Incomprehensible. This man had never had a penny more than necessary. What makes people so blind? As if whiskey could be anything other than a consequence of this system! Fortunately, I can also remind myself of Dr. Eleazar. 'I don't know,' he said, 'if I will ever be able to answer to my children in this "civilization" if I don't go to prison.' […]

Today – it is suddenly outrageously cold, in spite of the sun, and nobody knows what has come over the South – I drove through the lowlands to Montgomery, Alabama. Somewhere along the way, in a small Negro store, a young boy recounted the suffering: The white man owns the land. No work and no food.

The white man says you have to plant cotton. No corn and no vegetables. And if you have no money to buy them – how could you, given the price of cotton? – you just have to manage somehow.

And now I am ending this letter here in Birmingham. I could tell you much more. About the warm sun and my nose that has turned a deep red. About the trees that are already green here, and the cacti and palmetto. About the pink, red and white blossoms… not many yet, just a few. And about the inordinate hospitality and cordiality of the South.

Dr. Ernest Johnson's introductions and suggestions for my trip have been invaluable. Without him, none of it would have been possible. I would really appreciate your letting him know how much I am enjoying the opportunity he has given me.

Financially, I didn't do badly this month. That clearly points to California!

Chattanooga, Tennessee,
February 26, 1939

Dearest Mother,
Last evening, plowing through a torrential rainstorm in my little car, I felt the whole time as if I were coming home. So it was a bit of a disappointment to learn that Prof. Rollo Kilburn, who was holding my mail, lived quite a way out of the city and was too difficult to find. But this morning he came downtown with all my post [...] Letters from you, from Father, from Jaap, Ernst, Jochem, Anne, Dolph. I felt as rich as a king. [...]

Here in Chattanooga, I have left the South behind. I still have to take stock of that, but if anything has changed in the past few months, it is that I have aged a few years. I could write pages and pages about all the suffering, sickness, hunger and exploitation I have seen. But I will leave that. There is also the romantic South – lest we forget! – and a young and liberal South. [...]

Don't think it is just the problem of the Negro that has hit me so hard. It is also that of the poor white. And the laborer. It is frightful, a nightmare. In Birmingham – it was probably worse there than anywhere I have been up to now – I spoke to one of the higher-ups from US Steel. The man had a friendly face and we talked for an hour and a half. But what gibberish! [...] 'The unemployed worker is too lazy to do anything. Apart from that, there is no problem. The sharecropper is too lazy even to plant vegetables. He would rather lie in the sun for eight months. And after all, have you seen any of them dying of hunger? No, of course not.' Yes, well. [...]

I must underline one very important point here: almost everyone I have met is exceptionally friendly and warm-hearted. Unusually helpful and hospitable. Willing to give their time and whatever else. It is the wickedness not so much of the people as of the system. [...] In spite of everything I write I am growing to love these people more as each day passes. There is great courage, love of mankind (and a very genuine love of children), openness, and flexibility. Don't ever forget this! Johnson is looking after me as a father.

You haven't heard me complain in a long time, have you? Well, here goes: the YMCA is the most miserable, uninviting, uncomfortable and dirty institution in the United States. Even government politics are cleaner compared with the Y. I am wearing gloves because the table I write on is sticky from the dirt. I wear my clothes when I wash because even the air and the water in the washroom are foul. And this is true in every Y I have stayed in. They have all the shortcomings of a cheap hotel and are unfriendly as well. Even the people behind the desk are deaf. If I ever in my life have the chance to do something to bring about the demise of the Y, I will not fail to do so. Every so often I treat myself to a hotel room so I can take a bath. The one exception was my room in Atlanta. It was a little paradise. But the rest of the building stank to high heaven. [...]

Now to some comments in response to Father's letter of January 21, which has reached me only today. [...] I am afraid there is not much point anymore in sending you the text of Roosevelt's address because of the March 1 deadline for your article. The speech was printed in its entirety in the *New York Times* and I think that the university library in Amsterdam should have it.

On reflection, it seems to me that the hatred against England will not mean much in the event of war. My feeling is increasingly that America will join the war after about four months, at the very least by actively supplying arms. The aversion to Germany is very strong, but I continue to feel more and more that America must not enter in. First, the dislike of Germany could suddenly transform itself into blind hate. The Versailles Treaty was not nearly bad enough, etc. Secondly, and most importantly, 'America's fight to make the world safe for democracy' is a farce as long as 13 of the 48 states are semi-fascist or in any case completely undemocratic. That's America's first task. Only then comes its obligation elsewhere. No German will believe that America will go to war for democracy and not have another objective in mind. And it is very difficult to disagree with that point of view. I am sorry to say but the reason there is so much more discussion here of Germany than, say, of Georgia is because the former is not politically dangerous to talk about and the latter is. The principle is thus dead. The dangers in America are actually very great. Everything argues in favor of a forced and undemocratic transition from a price economy to a demand-driven economy. This is true for large areas of the US. For other areas, like California, it is not. Maybe that is sufficient to protect the country as a whole. In some places it is bad enough: Jersey City is, Louisiana was, just as fascist as Berlin or Bavaria.

I don't know if I mentioned to you what Miller wrote to me about the people surrounding Eleanor and Franklin D. Roosevelt. It was very disturbing. He is an ardent New Dealer – I don't have to tell you that. Briefly and without nuances, what he said was this: Roosevelt is an incredibly clever politician, Hopkins the most pronounced type of Lenin revolutionary I have ever met – unbalanced and, if need be, unscrupulous in his methods if it is for the good of the sacred cause. Cohen and Corcoran are medieval minions, Thurman Arnold a total fascist (Yes, Sir!). If Miller says this, it is well worth reflecting upon – the more so because countless New Dealers have said the same to me about Roosevelt. What is happening politically at the moment appears to be this: Roosevelt is trying to reconcile Big Business while at the same time treating conservative Democrats without any consideration. In other words, he is exposing his hidden opponents and at the same time undermining them. But it is very unlikely that he can pull this off sufficiently before 1940. As for the Republicans, my last hope in them was dashed when I heard from very reliable sources that Herbert Hoover was honest. Thus confirming my worst fears. In his case, he would be better off crooked than cricket.

[…]

PS End of the week: Knoxville and Norrisdam. Then West Virginia, Pittsburgh, and New York. Arrival around March 14. By then, the motorcar and I will have logged more than 5,000 miles. Up to now (4,000 miles), just a few flat tires. Not bad for $150. I am going to bed now; tomorrow I have to keep Professor Kilburn's class busy.

Knoxville, Tennessee,
March 8, 1939

[…]

This evening Arthur Ruper of the Southern Interracial Committee gave a talk here. You should have heard it! […] He galloped, leapt, flew and fell over words, sentences and parts of the talk. Jokes, gibes, asides. Suddenly deadly still, deadly serious. Then a passage from the Bible and, like thunderbolts, the wild indignant exhortation began all over again. Masterly! If America ever has concentration camps, he will be in one. But such a group of intensely pious devils can work wonders.

In Chattanooga I was a guest at a very interesting dinner hosted by Georg Fort Milton and his wife. He is one of the outstanding southern New Dealers. A typical Washington liberal, moderate humanitarian, with none of Ruper's zeal and religious background. Wealthy, hospitable, a lovely house – and appalling Negro shacks outside the door. A first-rate raconteur but, in the end, despite the charm and despite the lively, intelligent and attractive wife, powerless in his epicurean wisdom and a doomed man if the realities of life were ever to strike next door to his peaceful home.

In contrast, the meal yesterday with Kester, Smith and Nightingale in Knoxville was quite different. There was Kester, endowed with the refinement and culture that comes from an excellent upbringing and the insatiable fire that is necessary to keep someone in the church of the South. His wife was there as well with their sweet five-year-old daughter. He evangelizes and organizes in the Delta. Tarred and feathered in Oklahoma because of his interracial work and because he made it impossible for plantation owners to let people work in the cotton fields for only 30 cents a day. What courage must his wife have as well, never knowing whether he will return alive from his trip.

And there was Smith, who works for the cooperatives in the mountains, with his deep religious conviction that the cooperative movement is the spiritual and economic salvation of the stripped and abandoned hillsides, bereft of soil, the people in absolute poverty and despair. For them the cooperative is not self-help but perhaps a way to get away from the destructive spirit of American capitalism. Smith is quite hopeful because he works in mountain areas with excellent human material and because the cooperatives in so many places are able to return poverty to normal levels from their current lethal ones. Kester is more somber because he works in the midst of racial hatred and the murderous influence of a church that has forgotten its origins and aims as much as the Christians in Germany have.

Here in Knoxville (in the church of Reverend Nightingale) I confess to having given my second 'sermon'. This time, it was noticeably more tiring than in Chapel Hill, because after five weeks in the South, I can't get away with talking only about Germany. And there are more pleasant things to do than lecture a group of Southerners about what you think of racism in general. I phrased my questions as carefully as possible and Nightingale's well-raised (after fifteen years) congregation was exceptionally nice. After the service there was only one woman who came over to tell me, quite vehemently and angrily, that I had better first understand the South and that the Negroes have no better friends that the whites. [...]

Another important thing was that I got to see several quite depressing sides to New Deal endeavors: political scheming, bungling and trifling with people. The importance was that it clearly demonstrated how unbelievably complex the problems are, and how great the difficulties for the federal government. The productive economy is almost the best one can think of. The distribution system is finished on the drawing boards. But to hook up one to the other seems impossible to me. The only way open for democracy appears to be the slow, difficult and gradual changing of old and deeply rooted habits through schooling and persuasion. [...]

The abrupt swing to the right of the Administration and the mounting national debt – aggravated by the concern about this rise – do not mean, in my opinion, that the economic theory of the New Deal was incorrect but rather, how intense the mental resistance is to any kind of cooperative as opposed to some form of competition. The question arises with everything I see here: To what extent is it possible within the existing system to introduce changes little by little? Take the tenant farmer. You can teach him soil conservation and run electricity lines to his house. Say he conserves his soil and installs electricity. The value of his land and house increases. The next year he will have to pay more rent… or be homeless. Changing the system in states where the tenant does not have the right to vote is hardly likely. In the mountains, the aim is to set up cooperative stores. But if the retail chains come in for a few months to ruin your business or the wholesalers refuse to deliver to you, what then? Here again, it appears that it is not the merging of the profit and non-profit systems that is impossible but rather the peaceful acceptance of the mentality behind the two systems. If that is not possible, there will be bloodshed. [...]

Student of Amsterdam University Speaks Here

Max Kohnstamm of Amsterdam University, Amsterdam, Holland, visited the Cumberland Homesteads and was the week-end guest of A. Nightingale, speaking at the Congregational church on Sunday morning, March 5.

He has been in America four months on a traveling fellowship and will be here until September visiting interesting places in America.

He centered his address about the words—"Peace, Freedom and Justice." He said that in Europe they had no meaning for these words today as they were applied in their normal setting only to the privileged groups. He said that until these words implied for all people, regardless of creed, race or nationality in America and all over the world the meanings that Jesus put into them, they meant nothing.

Mr. Kohnstamm had a remarkable vocabulary for a man who had been in America only four months but explained that English is one of the required courses in all high schools in Holland.

Ermelo,
March 19, 1939

[Two days before the official entry of the German army into Prague; the army had already marched into Czechoslovakia on March 15.]

Dear Son!
A quiet hour on a Sunday afternoon in my cottage. Everyone is away. Next to me is your letter of March 8 from Knoxville. And in front of me is the news that now Romania has called upon England and France for assistance to stand up to German aggression and has mobilized five divisions. By the time you receive this letter, we will know whether this means war before Easter or whether we will still have a few months of preparation. But more about that later. First, I want to reply to your recent letters.

I am struck hard by your reports of the social and economic misery in the South. Of course, I had read and heard various accounts of it, but I had not imagined its extent and I had never thought that, given the prosperity, there could still be such backwardness in a country as immensely wealthy as America. It makes me better able to understand why precisely the Americans in the 'economic' section of the Oxford conferences[28] were so fixated on the organizing of industrial output and so unable to understand the question of what to do if we have a society that provides everyone with the comforts of life based on a three-hour workday? How will people be able to stand it?

What I cannot reconcile is your description of the situation – which must be the same for many millions of people, must it not? – with Roosevelt's program requirement of $1,000 annual income per capita in the near future. With a planned economy, this is of course achievable within one generation. But from what you say, the output in vast areas of the South must also be way below

---

28. In July 1937 two post-World War I ecumenical movements – Life and Work and Faith and Order – held world conferences at Oxford and Edinburgh, respectively. They decided to merge into one organization. In 1939 the first general assembly of what was to become the World Council of Churches was set for August 1941 but the war intervened, delaying the founding of the WCC until August 1948 when the first general assembly finally took place in Amsterdam.

average. Is the cotton unsaleable? Is much of it dumped, and doesn't anyone know how to replace the former cotton export with food products? A shortage of clothing in the land of cotton is surely unthinkable, is it not? From your letters, I can't make out whether the material suffering you describe refers to malnutrition or to slum dwellings. The last is, of course, only possible if there is a lack of understanding; with a decent housing policy, this situation should be able to be eliminated within one generation. Or is it primarily a problem of deforestation and as a consequence, soil deterioration?

This letter will reach you when you are back in New York. If you can, you must really try to share your impressions of the South with Reinhold Niebuhr of Union Theological Seminary, the author of *An Interpretation of Christian Ethics; Moral Man and Immoral Society* and *Reflections on the End of an Era*. In Oxford he was one of the people in the aforementioned economic section. He considered himself and his report very progressive; my objection was that he overestimated the influences of the social environment and economic production as opposed to those of psychological resistance and problems of overproduction. But the *Interpretation* is certainly a respectable book (the other I only know by title). Johnson can probably introduce you to Niebuhr, otherwise Sloane Coffin certainly can.

I still have a question regarding material need: what standard of comparison are you using? Have you ever observed, as carefully as you have in the South, the slums of Amsterdam or our turf huts? I am afraid that much of what you would find would not measure up to your expectations. Or is it really true there, and thus comparable to Brugman's description of the Dutch laborer around 1840 and other later surveys (of child labor, for example)?

But no more about that for now. Just one comment as a stepping stone to what I want to say next. The conditions that you describe appear to me to be the same in America as they are here, despite our outlook on life. I don't mean to whitewash, but it indicates a path people can take – and the Fellowship of Southern Churchmen does take – towards improvement. Even if it means being tarred and feathered – I had thought this no longer existed –

there is still the possibility for free speech and a free press. Even your 'sermon' did not put you in any danger of a concentration camp.

The dictatorship ideology practices consciously and with a leave-it-as-it-is intent its policy of oppression. Hitler has now dropped his mask of 'people's liberator'. Given all the grief of the past week, that is at least an improvement. And Chamberlain's speech[29] has confirmed my September impression of him that he was really serious about his right-wing convictions and restoration-of-Versailles efforts. As a result, I expect that what was postponed in the fall will now happen. After this unmasking, waiting any longer for the Berlin-Rome-Tokyo trio is not only pointless but also harmful because every month of waiting means a loss of advantage. A coup such as the one of March 15, if directed against Holland and Belgium, would almost certainly enjoy an initial success. The more the true meaning of the ideology of violence penetrates the slow-witted brains of the English and the Americans – not to mention ours – the less chance it has of succeeding.

This week the lower house of the British Parliament is debating how to organize the resistance by means of agreements with all the non-violent countries (including Russia!). It won't yield any results yet. The democratic countries are not yet mentally mobilized. Technically speaking, it is complete folly to wait any longer than May at the latest (for example, to organize Memel and the corridor[30]) because dictatorships lend their strength from assuming they can eliminate all considerations based on morality, decency and conscience. And to hope for another poker victory is almost out of the question (except, of course, for Memel and Danzig). For Hitler, however, there is no way back. He would also not see the need since he has never understood anything of England's indulgence of his earlier deeds. A short time ago, Herbert – who was also fooled – recounted the incredible stories

---

29. Speech held after the German occupation of Prague.
30. The northern city of Memel and the surrounding region and corridor of Memelland on the Baltic Sea were taken from Germany after World War I and brought under the jurisdiction of Lithuania in 1924. Lithuania was forced to return the district to Germany on March 23, 1939.

of a senior official in the foreign affairs department in Berlin about how easy it would be to overrun the morally depleted and emasculated West.

You see that my prognosis is not optimistic, at least with regard to the onset of war. I think differently about its end. Although it is of course true that God's ways are different from ours, I still cannot believe that his path would travel the route of the triumphant world imperialism of the New Heathenism. But it is pointless to conjecture.

What has been keeping me very busy these days is, of course, the question of whether I should give you advice about what to do and, if so, what it should be. And I have reached this conclusion: Come back. To stay in America forever? I cannot see that as your task. This morning at breakfast I read Matthew 16, 21–26 and Romans 8, 35–39 and I had you in mind as well.[31] What would be the use of your being in America if all hell breaks out here, unless you see a task for yourself in America that is directly related to organizing the resistance?

And even if war does not break out immediately, does it still make sense to prolong your stay by much? For me it is out of the question that we, even in the best of circumstances, will find ourselves returning to untroubled waters. Is it not a danger, in such unsettled times, that you will not have experienced in any of it? Will your return not seem strange and won't you find it difficult to catch up if you have let these months go by unproductively? This last concern also applies, in my view, in the highly unlikely event that the dictators pull back. But even discounting all of the above, I wonder if a California trip makes sense now, given your powerful experiences of recent months. You can't keep endlessly soaking up impressions. If you could find the opportunity in New York, or at Harvard, to develop your social and economic ideas, probing more deeply into them, discussing them with those who are also familiar with them – and thus better able to understand your passionate search for a solution than Europeans who have no answers based on observation – then I

---

31. Reading aloud from the Bible at the Sunday morning breakfast table was customary in many Protestant families.

think from the point of view of your study and education, it would be desirable and beneficial. But to gather still more impressions elsewhere – is there any point in that? If, as I would hope and expect, they are more favorable, you might risk losing the bitter aftertaste of the South if you don't go into it more deeply. But is that an advantage? And if, for example, you discover that the California oil industry and Hollywood are morally just as bad (Hollywood would certainly be better off materially!), what have you gained? In any case, a sort of sightseeing trip with Ernst seems to me to fit badly with the tenor of your recent letters.

These then are my views. I am certainly not losing sight of the fact that I am at a great distance and writing with very little knowledge of the details. Thus I can do little else than to clarify for you my thoughts about things as I see them.

And no human intelligence is capable of predicting the future with any kind of certainty in a world that has been turned upside down by lunatics. May the Lord grant you strength and certitude in answer to your questions to Him.

And so, until we meet again at His time,

Father

New York City,
March 27, 1939

Dearest Mother,

Outside the rain is falling. March. The South seems infinitely far away, a strange and provocative dream of beauty and rage, of human glory and human misery. [...]

Charleston, West Virginia, was awful – and so were the coal camps. Sinister, dirty, without a trace of beauty, clinging to the steep hillsides in a wasted valley – the only distinction between the houses and those of the Negroes being that the latter are a bit worse. And whatever makes life bearable in the South was missing.

When, to make matters worse, my car had to go to the garage for a minor problem, which cost me time, and the hotel in Morgantown, West Virginia, was miserable and the weather dreadfully cold, I decided to flee. But decisions don't count for much if you are dealing with the Klairs. And Reverend and Mrs. Klair kept me so intensely busy for four whole days in that dump of a town that I had to resort to schemes to be permitted half an hour to make my notes. They are totally crazy and the most delightful people I have met so far. A young married couple, two children. The upshot was four precious, silly and at the same time highly interesting days. [...]

Pittsburgh, in contrast, demonstrated to me that these big industrial centers will be a hard nut to crack. I feel too unhappy in such places to form a good impression. The city is so needlessly dreary, ugly and dirty. To have to spend an entire weekend there was just too much. [...] So instead I drove through Pennsylvania – in parts, very pretty with fertile, rolling countryside, solid old farms and beautiful barns; and in other parts, destroyed by the coal mines.

Then there is the international situation. In the days immediately following the invasion of Czechoslovakia I felt a great bitterness inside of me. Now it seems I am becoming accustomed even to this... and it all seems a little bit less dreadful now that England is at least starting to talk. Let us never forget that it took Chamberlain – according to the American newspapers – at least two days to become angry. There are so very many sides to the situation; an evening in Ermelo would possibly further my thinking but for now, a few comments.

First, from this vantage point, the situation is beginning to look as if it is moving towards a resolution. Tonight the newspapers are reporting the start of a press campaign against Poland. This all looks so pathological that we may be able to derive some hope from that. No Caesar can keep up the pace of two triumphal processions a week. [...] The worst of it – and the most somber – is the hopeless complexity and malignancy of the situation created. Without a word, England has admitted to its unforgivable September error. The safety of us all – the only safety of any value – hasn't even been defended in words.

Secondly, Daladier is turning France into a dictatorship. It is very clear that the war, if it comes, will be waged not because a man possessed by the devil is trampling on justice but because the interests of England and France have been negatively affected in an unacceptable way. It is the English-French status quo that is at stake, nothing else. Daladier and Chamberlain may have other motives – although I don't believe it – but they do nothing to make that clear to the Americans – and that is very much needed at the moment.

Thirdly, there is a strong movement here – on the rise since September – not to stand up for England's interests. By analogy, they point to Spain and China: If we really want to stand up for what is right, why didn't we do something then? For the American people the situation is becoming increasingly obscured by complex political factors and an arms program that nobody knows whether it serves to defend the coastline or European democracy. Add to this an ignorance of the European situation, the horrible memory of the World War, and an inherited optimism – now fading – that renders a real understanding of the Nazi philosophy impossible and you will see how confused and without direction the Americans are in face of the huge problem bearing down on them.

The conclusion seems frighteningly clear: the problem will not lend itself to a conscious, measured solution but, like an avalanche, sweep America along with it. The chances that it will drag America into war appear to be very great, but I fear that the consequences will be lamentable. War is terrible but if a nation does not understand why it is waging war or if it truly wants war or is simply being pulled into it, then the chances of a reasonable peace are slim. It is not so much the fact that America may well enter the war that disturbs me but that there is nobody, Roosevelt included, who knows precisely – and dares to say so – what the state of affairs is, what they are for or against, what principles are followed, which ideals are to be saved and which sacrificed. It is a very regrettable and ominous situation.

I keep coming back to the same conclusion: what we need more than anything is clarity about what the stakes are, at least to the limited extent that it is possible. To strive to understand everything and present it in the best possible light – what we have always been told is our Christian duty – must be thrown over-board. I know this is not easy, especially for Father! But there is one thing we have a right to and that is to get to see as clearly as possible the terrible problems with which the world is wrestling. That's why the September lies were probably far worse, far more dangerous than the March brutality... and hence, Chamberlain may be more evil than Hitler. I am not arguing for cruelty in my judgment of people but if you expect my generation to continue to find our way in the suffocating fog of uncertainty, vagueness and lies, then you must help us now to sharpen our convictions. There are times when it is a shame not to try to bring people together, to bridge differences. But this time it seems we are compelled to do the exact opposite. You well know that this is not the position I prefer to take. [...] If you don't agree at all, we can talk about it again in Ermelo.

New York,
April 3, 1939

[In a letter of March 17, Max's mother asks him about his plans for the summer in response to his proposal to travel to California together with his friend Ernst van der Beugel, who would come over especially for the trip. She wrote:

> Ernst phoned to say that you had asked him if he wanted to take a trip with you during the summer months. I had to brush away a sense of disappointment. Not so much because you would be coming home later than planned but because Father and I find it quite important for your well being that you get back to work and finish your studies rather than doing still more sightseeing with Ernst. But quite quickly the thought prevailed that we had to leave that decision up to you and, thank God, could leave it up to you.]

Dearest Mother,
Sometimes, now and then, there is a presumptuousness in older people that makes one wonder. I should indeed 'get back to work' tomorrow, rather than the next day, had I done any sightseeing at all. If staying up all night on a weekly basis to write up my impressions is not sufficient, then I must indeed possess a powerless pen.

Hall in Max's parents home in Ermelo with writing desk of his mother

America is – and I would really like you to try and understand this from my letters – a pretty overwhelming experience for me. I am looking at the country's social structure as through an immense magnifying glass. As a result, I am confronted as never before with the living monsters of society: human misery, the unutterable failings of our society, devastating greed and hatred. But there is also a group of dragon-slayers who are fighting with great courage what, I am afraid, is a losing battle. Seeing this happen has made a very strong impression on me. And I want to let it really sink in.

Then there is the very pertinent question: how will I view Holland when I return? I know nothing of the 400,000 unemployed – I have never seriously spoken to one of them. Here, yes. I know nothing of housing conditions there. I found Het Kolkje and the Burgwallen pretty.[32] The slums here are not pretty. But I wouldn't mind posing the question in Holland of what the people who live in those houses think about it. At the end of every sentence in every letter I write describing America, you have to think to yourself: What is the situation in Holland? What are our shortcomings? What should we do? And I am now convinced that the situation in Holland is far better, far healthier than here. But as long as there is one child who cannot go to school because it has no shoes, so long as there is one street in Amsterdam where people die younger than people on the upscale Apollolaan, there is no reason not to – as they say here rather pointedly – raise hell about it.

People in Holland don't slay dragons. Father has done it his entire life in the educational arena. My admiration of that is very great. But the voice of the dragon-slayer in Holland often sounds overstated and ridiculous. If I remember correctly, people have said that about Father's voice. And now I have to know more, before I leave here, about the powers at work in a capitalistic society, about the duty to slay dragons or not. And whether to do it in Holland or not.

[…]

Finally, a citation from Niebuhr: 'If Barth had arrived at his

---

32. Canal area in the center of Amsterdam, at that time impoverished.

present convictions ten years earlier, the history of central Europe might have been different, considering how powerful his influence was in accentuating those tendencies of Lutheranism which make it politically neutral.; However interesting as a hypothesis, I don't believe Barth was truly in a position to have prevented the unfolding of events.

New York,
April 6, 1939

Dear Father,
There is still no war. But the chances for peace seem virtually nil. I have postponed answering your long and loving letter of March 19, which made me very happy, hoping to gain some certainty first of my direction – one way or the other – during these days of terrible, tiring waiting, so reminiscent of the September weeks. But I am not going to wait any longer; your sketch of the situation appears to me to be completely correct and not too somber. It seems that only a miracle can save Europe. There appears to be no doubt about the outcome of the war. But then what? Here there is little reason for optimism. I think the intervention party will gain the upper hand, even despite Chamberlain's staying on as Prime Minister (again an unforgivable English blunder, according to public opinion in America). It is composed of very different groups, whose motives vary from noble to shabby. The tragedy of such situations is that in the long run it is usually the ignoble motives that predominate. And what sort of peace would that mean? [...]

I increasingly believe that even we young people will never again see a normal world. Furthermore, political reflections are no longer very useful now that the decision can come at any hour. Your letter arrived just as I had completed a long letter to you outlining my plans and poking a bit of fun at Mother's remarks about sightseeing. This week it was quite impossible and a bit half-crazy to make plans but I had to give it a try anyway. If war (or the mobilization of troops) occurs, I will of course come back. Only the embassy in Washington could change that, for example if it should want to use me here for whatever reason. As for staying here now in a period of 'calm', I am not afraid of becoming estranged because I have not participated in the events in Holland. On the other hand, it seems to me – given my September experience – pretty well impossible to make these times productive in Holland, although I admit that I will probably have to adjust myself to that. If there is any direct work to do – political, social, NCSV,[33] etc.– then this is a different matter entirely. If it only has to do with completing my studies, I don't regard a loss of ± two months as very serious.

As to the benefits of staying here: after the South and a bit (not more) of New York, I ought to experience one more 'real American' situation, if I am to be able to understand this country, to talk about it and eventually to write about it. Everyone tells me that. Therefore, after due consideration, I think it would be good to spend one or two months in the Midwest after a short visit to New England. Whether I then come home at the end of June or continue to travel until the end of August will depend on how much luck I have on this trip. If it becomes solely sightseeing – and as far as I am concerned there has not yet been one single day of that – then I will certainly not prolong it. That is to say, I will not go any farther after the Midwest. I have to write Ernst about one thing and another and I will advise him not to come, primarily because I have the feeling that one must undergo the enormous experience of America alone, not together with a friend.

About my lack of resolution, I am not going to do the work in New York after all. Six weeks of new impressions of misery in the summer would be more that I could handle, I think. And even if the danger of sightseeing threatens, I would not be averse to allowing the wide open spaces of the West restore to me some of that old 'Hope in America!' [...] But I would very much enjoy hearing from you again about this because, while Johnson may have my best interests at heart, talking something over quietly seems to be impossible in New York!

A few final remarks about the South. Miller told me today that

---

33. A liberal Protestant student organization.

nowhere in the Balkans had he seen anything as bad as in the South. This doesn't make the miseries of our turf hut farmers and slum dwellers any better, I must grant you that. […] The dreadful conditions here are malnutrition, lack of clothing, lack of education, and slum housing. The reasons are manifold. The soil is depleted because the tenant farmer does not stay on his land for more than one year. He has no money, no supervision and no reason to use fertilizer. He can't sell his cotton and he can't afford to buy cotton shirts. Most of the time the sharecropper is not permitted to plant anything other than cotton. Furthermore, he doesn't have the know-how and start-up capital to grow vegetables or keep pigs and cows. This situation exists on several million farms. The complex mechanisms that are crushing the South are difficult to describe in a letter. But the landowner system, now that I think of it, is the chief offender. In the cities, the slums are being maintained because they are a good investment at 15–20% return – sometimes even by the Church. The federal government is not allowed to build houses for people if they are able to pay rent because then the state would be competing with private enterprise. Nor is it allowed to build houses for people who are totally down and out and unable to pay anything because that would be contrary to its economic convictions. Hence, cleaning up the slums is an extremely long process and every inch of ground won has been fiercely fought for. Moreover, it is true that people who have lived for generations in slums cannot simply be transferred to new homes. The South should, under good management, certainly be in a position to feed the entire population. […]

I do agree with Niebuhr that for the time being, a three-hour workday is not needed in America. I think you will fully understand his position if we discuss these things again and in greater detail when I am home.

I have on occasion attended the University Seminar. Heard Tillich lecture. It was of course very good. But it did not strike me as great, or of a distinction that I had not yet experienced. And very German. […] I don't think that I would want to stay here another year because of him. But maybe my impression of him is not quite correct. At the moment I am reading Richard Niebuhr's

(Yale) *Kingdom of God in America.* Top-notch.

I shall stop now. My letter will then be in time to sail with the Queen Mary [...]

Your Max

PS With regard to Chamberlain, the facts bear out your interpretation but I find it very difficult to believe in it.

Ermelo,
April 2, 1939

Dear Son!
Mother has already written you at length, so you will understand this penciled note from bed and I needn't dwell on it further.

As I write, you are probably already in New York and in receipt of my letter of a fortnight ago. I want to return to that briefly. With Hitler's Wilhelmshafen response to Chamberlain's declaration in front of us, we can probably say now that this time the poker game will not be continued and further menacing will be postponed.[34] As a result, the most pressing reason for you to come back has been eliminated and thus I suspect your decision in that regard has already been taken. Nonetheless, the question of your future plans still needs to be considered and we of course look forward with great interest to your news about that.

My views on your trip to California and the West with Ernst have changed little since March 17. But I am quite willing to give you credit for the correctness of your decision. Far better than unplanned travel would be to arrange to meet people who could foster western cooperation, which is becoming more urgent by

---

34. On March 31 Chamberlain pledged that Britain and France would guarantee the independence of Poland. The next day, April 1, Hitler held a speech in the German port of *Wilhelmshafen*, on the occasion of the launching of a battleship. According to The New York Times of April 3, 'It was a truculent speech [...] but it proposed no immediate action [...] and it refrained significantly from any ultimatum to Poland.' Although Hitler asserted that 'Germany has no intention of attacking other people', *The Times* of London on April 3 said that the speech 'was clearly bitter and threatening, particularly against Britain's efforts to protect Eastern European states from Germany'.

the week (because Hitler's pronouncement of only wanting to serve the cause of peace cannot, of course, be believed).

I am quite impressed by a book I have just finished reading: Clarence K. Streit's *Union Now: a Proposal for a Federal Union of the Leading Democracies*. It is very radical indeed and probably too perfect to be practicable. Nonetheless, Streit is probably right that it is the only way out of the impending world catastrophe. The author is clearly a man with a very broad outlook and deeply rooted in the American tradition of Washington and Lincoln, in the principles of the Bill of Rights. And you well know how precious those are to me. I will probably write to Streit myself shortly because he asks for letters of endorsement. If you see an opportunity to talk to him personally and inquire about what further steps he is proposing to take, it would interest me very much. I would also be interested in your impression of him as a person. He lives in Washington at 1 Second Street, NE.

I hope by now that your power of attorney for notary Ludwig is under sail. Because if it still requires Mother's last letter or this one to prod you to do it, it will arrive too late. In this regard, how is it that I have never heard a thing from you in response to all my earlier questions? An unnecessary tax payment of $\pm$ 600 guilders is not the worst thing that can happen in these times – I could consider it as a voluntary contribution to spend on our national defense and social security benefits – but on the other hand the requests for support from all sides are so numerous and urgent that the thought of having to pay this amount simply because the due date has passed is annoying, particularly when I tried to settle it all so early.

If you still decide to go to California, let me know in advance so I can give you an introduction to Ralph Tyler Flewelling, director of the University of Southern California at Los Angeles School of Philosophy and publisher of *The Personalist*, for which I am one of the foreign advisory editors. He will certainly receive you cordially and, if you are in the vicinity, I think it would be a worthwhile visit.

With very much love,
Father

Ermelo,
April 20, 1939

Dear Son!
Mother sent you a postcard yesterday so its arrival may precede this letter with the good news that the diagnosis of a tumor has been pretty much ruled out. The days between Tuesday the 11th and today were, of course, curious. They made me – and, I am convinced, everyone around us – see clearly once again what are the true and what are the false values in life, and to feel an immense gratitude for the faculties given to us to make that distinction. For me it was also a test of whether I could adhere to the convictions I set down in the last chapter of *De Heilige* when death presents itself as no longer purely theoretical. And I am thankful to say that – up until now – this test was passed without difficulty.

Now I am sitting once again in the beautiful spring weather and writing to you with the genuine expectation of being able to return to work in May – and perhaps here and there help to do something useful to ward off the far more serious public danger. Here too – although we are still in the midst of uncertainty and without any means as simple as a blood sedimentation rate to give us certainty – it seems as if we are over the worst of it. By 'the worst of it', I mean not war but the capitulation of the entire world – one country after another – to the totalitarian madness because of egotism and indecision. I think we are still a long way from ruling out war or even the trampling underfoot of smaller countries and territories, including ourselves, of course. But these are questions of detail that cannot be calculated as long as the Caesarian madness holds sway in Berlin and Rome. But after Roosevelt's message,[35] I think we can pretty much rule out any possibility that it will achieve world dominance. And for that, we can be grateful to him… and Chamberlain.

I feel again strengthened in my conviction that Munich was not treason and that the policy not to declare war immediately in the wake of Prague and Albania was a difficult but wise one.[36] Just

---

35. See note 20.
36. The Italian army had invaded Albania on April 7, 1939.

this morning the newspaper is reporting the joint guarantee of Poland and Russia to the Baltic States. If this is true and the English-Turkish-Balkan attempts succeed, then the local danger has not been averted but the global danger certainly has. Typical in this respect are the changed reports coming from Japan and, best of all, the probably unexaggerated reports of Chinese recovery. May God grant that Canton will be the turning point.[37]

I am writing all these things under the fresh and powerful influence of Hermann Rauschning's *Die Revolution des Nihilismus*. It is the most intelligent and well-documented book on National Socialism that I have yet to lay my hands on. The author was an insider: National Socialist President of Danzig in 1934 and regional leader of the party. Under orders from Hitler, he negotiated, among other things, a personal meeting between the Polish President, Pilsudski, and Hitler to settle the question of Danzig. He represented Danzig in Geneva when Germany resigned from the League of Nations. His book seems to me to be the most authoritative contribution to collective psychopathology that I have ever seen, the more so because the author does not propound psychological theories or pursue personal hobby horses but gives (in the main) the facts. He himself comes out of what can be called the Hindenburg[38] circle and was an active participant until 1934, when his eyes were opened to the monstrous devilry that, despite all its excesses, he had always considered a pardonable attempt to nullify the Treaty of Versailles. You must read the book, preferably soon; it is published by Europa-Verlag, Zurich-New York, and should be easy to find. Of course, I don't mean to say that I agree with everything the author says. When he writes about a completely 'doctrine-less Revolution', I think he sometimes underestimates the older National Socialists, especially Hitler himself, but even he (Rauschning) is very attracted to the *Staatsräson* and the amoral concept of power. But it is, in any case, a book that everyone who wants to be fully alert to these times

---

37. In the war between Japan and China, begun in 1937, the Chinese fought their first victory at Canton (Guangzhou).

38. Paul Hindenburg, famous German general in World War I, elected President of the Weimar Republic in 1925 and re-elected in 1932, but forced to transfer power to Hitler in 1933.

will have to have read.

This book and Roosevelt's action are also holding me back from writing to Streit, as I recently told you I would. I had not yet gotten around to it because it seemed foolish to write when the tumor diagnosis was still looking unfavorable. And at the moment I think that Streit's overly ambitious (although, in my view, good and non-utopian) plan would be in danger of evoking resistance that could delay and obstruct the most urgent and dire need to stop the aggression. Nonetheless, I abide by my recommendation to read the book and, if you can, to seek verbal contact with him. He is a man on the right track who knows a lot and dares to act as a matter of principle.

And now to your letter of April 6 (sent April 7, received April 13!). I read it with very great interest, first and foremost your explanation of the social and agrarian situations in the South. Therein clearly lies the core of truth in Henry George's and Oppenheimer's landownership theories. It struck me because I had just received a pamphlet about their liberal socialism, which seeks to explain all social and economic misery on the sole basis of large-scale landownership and an erroneous land-lease policy. That, of course – especially after the appearance of modern agrobiology – is naïve and one-sided because a sharecropper can't start up anything without current assets. But your letter makes abundantly clear that there are vast and still unsuspected areas where improper land use policies also govern the fundamental mistakes of our social structure. In that respect, I had become too strongly 'industrial' in my thinking so what you are telling me is a good correction.

As for Niebuhr: I too have never thought, let alone said or written, that within 50 years a three-hour workday somewhere in the world would become desirable or even necessary. But a world conference such as Oxford '37 must a) dare to examine things on the basis of principle (its theological participants especially must dare to do this) and b) keep in mind the very serious fact that a coming three-hour workday would take at least 50 years of psychological-pedagogical preparation in order to become beneficial. There is still, it seems to me, a strong, unexamined Marxism in Niebuhr and Tillich and a lack of training in scientific thinking. But we can talk about this later. What you further write about Tillich pretty much confirms my – not very considered – opinion about him. I am not familiar with [Richard] Niebuhr's *Kingdom of God in America*.

With regard to your prospective plans, I agree that it won't much matter to your future here whether you return before September or not, and that it is quite possible that the coming months could be very important to achieving consolidation and balance to your American impressions and experiences. [...] What the South has given you – and I hope for the rest of your life – is the burning interest and realization of the fact that you are indeed your brother's keeper. But what, without hubris and within practical and realistic parameters, your task will be in that respect can better be sorted out here than in New York. When it comes to social work, it seems to me that America at any rate – contrary to the large organizational questions like the New Deal – is not much further along than we are, and for concrete applications you still have to familiarize yourself with the realities here, unless you should decide to stay over there, which I wouldn't advise.

As for universities – your friendly references in your letter to Mother to study possibilities in Ermelo notwithstanding – I would like to say this: Philosophy in the broadest sense, including of course the burning questions of world issues – can probably be better and more thoroughly studied in Holland under expert guidance than somewhere in America. If your own field of study – which up to now is still history – would allow that, I don't know. As you may have noticed from our talks, my impression of Huizinga is much less deep than what is commonly thought.[39] However, the filling of the vacancy left by Brugmans has taught me that nobody here in Holland can measure up to him, let alone improve on him. If you could still spend a term at Harvard or Yale studying under someone of that caliber, I of course don't know. I am really thinking only of Rostovtzeff, who impresses me very much after what you have told me, and especially in a subject – modern history – in which I cannot serve as a guide, having no

---

39. Johan Huizinga (1872-1946), preeminent Dutch historian, professor of history at the University of Leiden.

detailed knowledge of the methodology. If you could still do that, I think it would be very important, even more important than the Midwest and West. But only on the condition that you can find such a mentor.

If not, I think you should follow Johnson's advice but, before you head west, first see something more of early New England, keeping this question especially in mind: What is still to be seen of Washington's (and Lincoln's!) spirit in the original confederation of states? Lincoln really has to be included here, even though I think he was born in Kentucky. Apart from that, do you really know him from close up? It would seem to me to be quite important to discover how much of the spirit of these two great men is still alive in America. I will not be easily convinced that there is very much left of it… up to and including Roosevelt's message. On the other hand, in this respect, Streit's interpretation would appear to me to be important; I regard him as more than a 'journalist'.

[…]

Well, this has been a lengthy letter, but it is now longing for an end. Let it be this: the thought of you and your impressions, experiences and plans was one of the many things that made me feel thankful, happy and at peace in recent weeks.

God be with you, my son!

Father

New York,
April 10, 1939

[*Max has not yet received the preceding letter from his father.*]

[…]

The reports here have been the same as in Holland, I think. Every so often (and especially yesterday evening) the newspapers discuss the possibility of a lightning attack on Holland. Today the direct threat seems to be a bit less. But tomorrow it may be different again. […] I will not come home unless there is mobilization or a specific task awaits me. The situation can turn into open war in three days or it can take six months or even longer. If Father and, for example, Dolph or Professor Scholten[40] think totally differently about this, I am open to their views and will – if you let me know by telegram – immediately head home. […]

But worse than the threat of war and the realization once again – as in September – that everything you ever hoped and dreamed for in life had to be surrendered was the hopeless unprincipled behavior of it all. Father simply cannot defend Chamberlain anymore. Albania makes me sick. I am fully aware that Zog was probably a scoundrel. But does statutory law not count for anything? It was – and that's good – the proof that England is still afflicted with blindness and could not care less about the collective security of international law. England's sole goal is to save the British Empire. Crass egotism, without a trace of guilt about having sold out the League of Nations, China, Spain, Abyssinia, Czechoslovakia, Albania. What next? And for this miserable clique, we are going to be shot and killed!

The war is not going to be for something – because nowhere is there a noble cause. It will only be against something. And there is reason to be against Germany. […]

In the newspaper I read that the Dutch Government has stated that the invasion of Albania was 'of no concern' to it. […] Our Christian Government finds it no business of theirs what happens on Good Friday in the rest of the world; at any rate, it is too scared to say anything about it […] By so doing, Holland gives up its right to existence! […] It is nothing more than a little club of haves who are deathly afraid of the have-nots. It is not a whit better than Germany, only wealthier. If tomorrow, German troops invade Holland, then it will be the self-evoked scourge of God and not a German wrongful act. […]

A fond embrace,

Your

Max

PS I don't want to conceal the fact that the making of plans is becoming complicated by the uncertainty about whether or not to go to the West Coast – in which not only scholarly but also

---

40. Paul Scholten, a very influential law professor at the University of Amsterdam and friend of Philip and An.

personal motives could play a role.

New Haven,
April 21, 1939

Dear Father and Mother,
Today I received Mother's grave letter of April 13 [*in which she tells Max about the serious illness of his father*].
　[…]
The Yale campus is serene and still and spring-like and I am reminded of our autumn day in Cambridge [England]. My heart goes out to you, to that beloved old creaking house. Sometimes when I would take a walk on a warm summer's night and see the lights burning in the bedrooms, or the house completely dark, I would ask myself whether the house was a part of me or whether I was just a part of the house.
　And now there is not only the threat of war, which has not really left us alone for the past year and a half, but above all, the tremendous worry about Father […] God grant that our fears are premature. […] As for me, if Dr. Holtrop's diagnosis is correct, I see absolutely no reason to prolong my stay in America. […] If you want to advise me by telegram not to come home, I would appreciate your talking it over first with Herbert or Dolph or Philip. The best way to reach me, after I have left Boston (April 29), will be via Washington.

Cambridge,
May 3, 1939

[…]
　It was such a strange weekend until the telegram arrived. I don't have to tell you how intensely happy I was to hear the news. […]
　Before I attempt to give you a short report on recent weeks and future plans, partly in response to Father's long, loving letter, I have one comment on the world situation. The direct danger

has perhaps faded for a few days, weeks, months – nobody knows – but Father's opinion, endorsed in simultaneous letters from Dolph and Anne, is wholly mine. Virtually all the dynamite is still there and nobody knows if and when it will explode.

It's crazy but I have gotten so used to the idea of war that really only one hope remains: to be allowed once again to see Schapendrift in peaceful times. […]

First impressions of New England: as a whole, vastly more 'European' than the South, even than New York. Yale also comes much closer to our universities as far as standards and spheres of interest are concerned. The professor-student relationship is totally different, however – mainly better. But there is the slightly disturbing question of academic freedom, of the huge influence of the administration on the lives and thoughts of students and faculty, and of the fund-raising side of it all. Rostovtzeff – as every American! – is unbelievably friendly, but too much of a classicist and not someone to whom you can say, 'I am coming to work under you for a few months.' [Richard] Niebuhr is terrific. A very, very impressive man. And with a modesty and an obliging character that put every young person – and certainly me – to shame. A very interesting discussion of political theory. I really hope that Father finds the time for his *Kingdom*, although Niebuhr is larger than his book. All of Yale Divinity School made my mouth water – much more than Union Theological Seminary. Now that you can't give me a present on my birthday, you may instead send Jo[41] (if he does his best on his exams) over here for a half-year. Seriously: money well invested.

New Haven, Boston… the problem of foreigners is very big here, as you know. New Haven is 60% Italian, Boston is run by completely corrupt Irish. The social-political situation is heavily influenced by language groups. Economically, the area is suffering from the shifting of industry to the South where, beyond the reach of labor laws, lower wages and longer hours promise higher profits. What can be done?

The farm question: The farm set-up as a whole is healthy,

---

41. Jo Pik, a theology student at the University of Utrecht and protégé of Max's parents.

although there are farms that took out impossible mortgages before the Great Depression. The Farm Security Administration has to deal with far more modest but no less difficult problems. But on the whole, the farmland here is good and the countryside looks beautiful. If I had such a farm, I would be a Republican too. In Boston I spoke to labor and Farm Security people, a journalist, and a Negro lawyer and visited the New England Student Christian Movement. I also attended a seminar at Harvard University. Eccles, the commander-in-chief of the 'spenders' gang and governor of the Federal Reserve System, came up from Washington. Extremely interesting! Perhaps most interesting was the feeling of utter hopelessness about ever getting anything done nationally [...]

Spent the weekend in Maine at a student conference on social action. An unusually pleasant and lively group. [...] Monday and Tuesday in New Hampshire and Vermont with the regional director of the Farm Security Administration. Tomorrow a visit to a typical mill town abandoned by industry. [...] The weather is distressingly awful. [...] If it does not instantly stop snowing, my next letter to you will be posted from California or Florida. [...] As for [Reinhold] Niebuhr and Union, I agree with him that America need not fear anything less than a six-hour workday for the next fifty years. The standard of living is so appallingly low. And in addition, there is an opportunity here that no European country has: a return to the land. Garden villages and subsistence farming. The tendency in the North-east is in this direction under the guidance of excellent Italian gardeners. On the whole, I think that the problem of leisure time is much easier to solve here than, say, in our country. There is a truth to be found in the great simplicity and naivety of the American.

With regard to finances, the car has behaved with great dignity. Pocket money brought from Washington combined with American hospitality have been sufficient up to now. Henceforth, however, I will have to withdraw about $125 a month. [...] As for my plans, I am beginning to think more and more about returning home around August 15, to let America sink in a bit, to give myself time to settle back into Holland again and to have something left of the summer to enjoy in Ermelo before setting out to finish my studies in September. But I will make that decision when I reach Chicago. [...]

Detroit,
May 17, 1939

[...]
It is becoming harder than ever to write at length about my wanderings. The things that keep me busy are less shocking and also less of a piece than the problems in the South, and it would take too long to explain this in a letter. Maybe the steadily approaching day of my homecoming also makes me lazier about writing. [...] The trip through the 'dead' towns of New England

– Manchester, Lowell, New Bedford, Fall River, etc.– was illustrative of how complex some problems here can be when the decline of capitalism accompanies the decline of regionalism. [...] Industry abandons New England in order to benefit from the lower wages in the South, leaving behind desolate towns in Massachusetts, Rhode Island, New Hampshire and Maine to build even more desolate mill towns in North and South Carolina, Georgia, Alabama and Mississippi.

I gather from some of the letters of my friends that people are getting worried and even angry about my over-hasty and wild conclusions. Fortunately, I have never had the feeling from any of Father's letters that you share this opinion. And I cannot see that the conclusion that something is unbearably wrong with the system is so rash or wild when at every step of the way you are confronted by hunger, unemployment and slums. [...] Nowhere in Holland will be too small or unimportant for me this year, and that includes the fraternities, hazing, the student council and whatever else, because everywhere it is all about people. Of course, there is a certain kind of Dutch pompousness – all the way up to the Royal Family – that seems a bit ridiculous in comparison with the behavior of the people, who are really in power on earth, as they are here in the United States. Eccles, for example, referred to Roosevelt's cabinet as 'the boys'. But what sends the blood rushing to my head every time, and what could ultimately drive me back to America, is the accursed small-mindedness of our Christian politics. [...] The selling-out of ideals and traditions. Bah, bah, bah. I wish I didn't find Holland so important because then it wouldn't bother me so much. [...]

At Smith College I talked at length with Els Elias[42] about what America has done to us both. [...] The reason I have come to love this country is the wide-openness to criticism, the forever raising of the question, 'What is wrong here?' And perhaps most important of all – despite the enormous political-economic questions – is a personal life that is appealingly uncomplicated. Plus the immense friendliness and the youthful, easy-going,

---

42. A history student from the University of Amsterdam and friend of Max who was also spending the academic year in the United States.

amenable [approach to life]. All of that can move me deeply.

After Smith, I drove in high spirits – spring is at its peak – across New York State to Oberlin College. En route I stayed in the home of an elderly couple. Formerly a Republican county boss, he is now an ardent New Dealer – and even well to the left of that. They were incredibly dear, delightful people, living in a lovely old New England home with antique furniture, old portraits and full of beautiful things. Fragrant flowering trees encircled the house. […] In the evening he read aloud to me from Walt Whitman. Beautiful. The old voice was so full of fire when he read the songs of love and freedom. *Pioneers! O Pioneers!* After each verse he would blow a little through his teeth and look away so no one could see how overcome with emotion he was. […]

[After visiting Oberlin, Max drives by way of Cleveland – 'a grim monument of protest against the social order' – and Ann Arbor to Detroit.]

It is always fascinating to enter a city, establish your contacts and then slowly start looking and listening – the facts are mostly contradictory! – in an attempt to form an impression of the people, the problems, the opportunities and the struggles. But after Detroit and Chicago, it has become clear to me today […] that I am not up to taking everything so seriously anymore. It is too warm and too much like summer to continue to have social feelings. I'm beginning to reach my saturation point. All of this is by way of preparing you for the fact that I have decided to go to California anyway.

[Max explains that he can sell his car in California for 'a horrendous amount of money'. Second-hand cars there are 'priceless', whereas in Detroit and Chicago you have to pay someone to take them off your hands.]

Detroit,
May 17, 1939

Dearest Mother,
A postscript about California, but only – and really only – to be read by you and Father. Take care: if you don't hold your tongue, you will pay for it later.

It is a little difficult to do this by letter but I really want you both to know something. I am going to California solely and exclusively for Jane. Do you remember Jane from my Washington letters? Jane came to mean a great deal to me there. On my last evening, we had a conversation that touched both of us deeply. I was too unsure of myself to ask her outright and, what was much more important, Jane told me very clearly that the differences for her were insurmountable. These differences – which I also felt were very great – had mainly to do with her being a Christian Scientist. In my deliberations for and against a trip to California, it slowly became clear to me that I was really only thinking about Jane. And I wrote her that. I received a very fine and frank answer that all but told me not to come for her sake. Because of that 'all but', I am going to go anyway. I don't think I can lose very much by going – because I am not afraid that a candid 'no' will kill me. And I do think that the uncertainty and the feeling of not having dared […] would continue to bother me. […] In such situations, prudence can mean either lack of courage or a wise move. So I am immensely looking forward to California and shall head west with a feeling of carefree abandon. […] I feel very sure of my ground. Not at all of Jane but of the correctness of my decision. […]

A very loving kiss from your Max

My dear son! Your letter of May 17 from Detroit calls for a word of reply, albeit a somewhat timid and reserved one given the incomplete information about what truly matters, about how you truly feel about each other. Nonetheless, your letter does provide a clue when you say that in Washington 'the differences were insurmountable' for her and now that she 'all but told you not to come to California for her'.

Because a few things are really very clear. You are certainly not yet, according to your letters, at the point of seeking your future in America. Such a decision – if you ever make it – should first be weighed carefully after your impressions of this year have settled and after you have renewed contact here and are in a position to draw comparisons. And to transplant Jane to Holland, in the current world situation, would be a very big responsibility. I can understand very well that she would feel this to be a sacrifice that she would not wish to make. Of course, with a deep commitment, consciously chosen, all manner of human calculations or reservations can be overcome, but your letter does not show that deep commitment – quite the opposite. I don't mean at all to imply that the two of you should or even could be ready for such profound decisions. All kinds of things still have to become stronger and more firmly rooted in you. But I would be very much mistaken if you were ever to become a confirmed Christian Scientist; I am inclined to think that you have too much of my outlook on science and religion for that. And the expectation that Jane, on the other hand, would grow into your way of thinking means that you are asking of her an even bigger change than that of country, people, language and familiar surroundings. For the moment, I would call her position nothing other than objectively correct and completely respectable. In any case, I would like to say this: definitely do not try to force a decision now in California. It seems to me to be your duty, as I said before, to let the experiences of the past year first settle before you commit yourself and especially before you interpret any eventual change in her stance as a binding decision on her part. If, when you see her in California, it turns out that she feels differently than her letter led you to believe, then that would wholly justify your trip but it would not justify a decision of such major consequences for both your futures. In any case, at least postpone a decision until you have taken more time on both sides to let it sink in. Otherwise, I would be worried that an inordinately romantic bias had not sufficiently taken into account the very real drawbacks to such a decision.

My dear son: May the Lord grant you counsel and wisdom that you will not want for strength.

Father

Chicago,
June 3, 1939

[…]
My last letter was sent from Detroit. The total picture there was hardly encouraging. Sharp class distinctions and class conflict. All the shortcomings of corporation police and spy systems, corrupt city police and city government. […] Add to all of that an enormous unemployment and a good dollop of anti-Semitic propaganda. A perfect pre-fascist set-up.

I have now been in Chicago for about ten days. I am living in a sinfully luxurious suite with a view of the lake, bathroom, etc. It is so mercilessly and relentlessly hot here that I couldn't stand those stuffy, dark, cheap hotel rooms any longer. Chicago is tremendously American and I feel infinitely more at ease here than in New York. But the corruption is pretty appalling – corruption in the city government with branches in the underworld and labor unions. One of the people at the University of Chicago put me in touch with a fabulous old boss in the milk drivers' union, a gang of out-and-out racketeers. He earns $13,000 a year, but complained that he had to fork out so much to others, especially to the police, that there wasn't much left. The president of their union was kidnapped several years ago, causing my friend to go out and buy a bulletproof car. He proudly showed me the now ancient and useless carcass in the garage. Every room in the house was bulletproof. After the kidnapping, they murdered five gangsters without any interference from the police. 'We are not gangsters – we are good citizens. But these people who get tight and kill decent people. They kill decent people, don't you see?'

It would be hilarious if it were not so costly to the city government. This is one of the reasons that Chicago's slums are more extensive and much worse than in any other Northern city. The wretched, filthy, gray misery defies all description. More or less the same is true of the stockyards. But I didn't faint. I have met a couple of terribly nice young journalists here – and I am always amazed at how good these journalists are, even though they work for rotten newspapers. […]

Roosevelt is ready to collaborate with everyone if it appears politically necessary. That a man like Kelly – the chief of the completely corrupt Chicago machine – is one of the New Deal propagandists for a '3rd term for Roosevelt' is, to put it mildly, disagreeable. A second thing that interests me here is the political conviction of the large, very powerful Farm Associations that have their headquarters here. […] There is a growing aversion to the labor movement […]. Dr. Taylor, director of the Farm Foundation, told me that what America needed was a government that would dare to discontinue all relief payments. It is incomprehensible that he does not see what the result of this would be. Everything goes by the motto: the farmer has to make his labor available in the free labor market because the price of farm products is not controlled. Conversely, the labor union is a wage monopoly that stabilizes the price at a level at which the farmer cannot purchase. 'So, starve the labor man to death.' Poor America, if these types gain supremacy in 1940.

Meanwhile, I am beginning to scout around travel agencies in Chicago and inquire about ships. When I write you my next letter, I may already know on which day in August I will be quitting these shores. […]

Madison, Wisconsin,
Sunday, June 11, 1939

Mother dearest,
Wednesday, August 9, at 12 p.m. the *Washington* departs from the pier in New York to bring me home! And precisely one week later I will be in Ermelo. I looked into a variety of possibilities, including freighters from Montreal and New Orleans, but they all took too long. So I finally decided to go ordinary third class. It is quicker and not much more expensive. [...] The boat trip is a pain in the neck anyway so why pay $40 more [to travel second class]. The ship docks at Plymouth on the evening of August 18 and the following morning at Le Havre, which means I can be home on the same day! [...]

I will nose around here in Wisconsin, Iowa and Kansas until July 5. From July 5 to July 12, my address will be c/o Presbyterian Summer Conference, Fairfield, Iowa. Yes, I will be a 'class teacher': 'Looking toward a better world.' Don't laugh [...] From there I will travel by car to California, where my address will be 345 Kellogg Avenue, Palo Alto. Around August 1, I will return to Washington to pack up. [...]

The brief visit [of England's King George VI] is a great success and I am enjoying reading the accounts of it in the newspapers. The typical form of address: 'Hullo, King.'

Chicago was very hot – it got so hot, in fact, that I began to ask myself how much longer I could bear it. [...] Here in Madison, a magical city between the lakes, it is cooler. We have just had two really cold, rainy days, so I am now longing again for warmth. In Chicago I began my survey of farmland and I will try to continue that here. The November elections brought anti-New Deal results in the Midwestern and North-western states, mainly as a result of the swing in the farm vote. [...] For the continued existence of the New Deal – or any other liberal group – it is of enormous importance how the farm-labor relationship develops further.

Until now, Governor Heil – while his name conjures up dangerous associations – appears to be more ludicrous than dangerous. But how would that be on a nationwide scale? Detroit and Chicago have not made me more optimistic. In Chicago, in the vicinity of the beautiful university, in the glorious parks along the lake, I kept feeling the threat. You know how the outskirts of a city can be on hot, summer afternoons. Hardly a soul on the street and only the sound of someone somewhere playing a piano. That was Chicago, at least in the vicinity of the Broadview Hotel and the International House where I later stayed. But beyond it all: the wasteland, the blighted areas – forgotten and forsaken. It was a bit like dancing on a volcano, this sunny student life around the Midway and the lake in summer. [...] And the question keeps arising of whether in this political system, this society, anything can be done about it? Or is the stage of fascist or communist revolution inevitable? Chicago is certainly no signpost for democracy...

And here I sit, for the time being, in the cold and in of a burst of already much regretted economizing in a YMCA that beats the lot for dreariness and dirt. Conversely, Madison is a little jewel and Wisconsin an unbelievably beautiful state. A little bit like Limburg, but with many, many lakes.

Des Moines, Iowa,
June 25, 1939

My dearest Mother and dear Father,
My window frames the warm, dark Iowa night. It is late and the sluggish heat of the day makes me long for bed. But I feel a peacefulness within me and a need to talk to you [...] As I sit here writing after a difficult day of reflection, the heat still lingering around me and the crickets as loud as they are on hot summer days in Ermelo, I only have to close my eyes and I am there: the lawn in the warm night, the birches, and the lamps burning in your bedroom, reminding me of the lights on the bridge of a ship. [...]

So much is hypothetical, unreal, because California and Jane are so recently out of the picture. [...]

Next to me is a copy of *Life* magazine with photos of how men died in 1914–18 and how they die now... and maybe will in the future. And ahead of me, the enormous night that is descending over the world. Do you know, my dearest Mother, that in your reply to my letter telling you that I had perhaps found someone who wanted to share my loneliness, there was not a single word of rejoicing over what for me would have been such great joy? [...]

PS Sunday afternoon
I am enclosing the last note from Jane that will tell the story better that I can, and also an earlier letter, both of which I hope to have returned to me. I don't yet know what I will do next. It is very difficult to give up California at this point but it will have to happen. I will be in Fairfield, Iowa, until July 12 and after that at my old address in Washington.

Monday, June 12, 1939
Dear Max,
I have news of a sort for you: I have a job! It doesn't begin right now, exactly, but it will next fall or in January when Spencer and I are married. Does that surprise you? It certainly did me. I had not expected that to happen at all, but this last week it did – all of a sudden. And here I am. [...]

Des Moines, Iowa,
July 2, 1939

[...]
As for me, I have given up on ever being able to attain the enviable state of manhood. Someday I'll wake up to the fact of being in it. And then maybe it won't be fun anymore. It is the same sad story as with the streetcar. Before we moved out of Amsterdam in 1926, it was my great dream to be allowed to ride on the front platform of the streetcar, only without anyone seeing anything strange in it. When I returned to the city from the woods seven years later, the unattainable ideal was achieved, but the dreamed-of satisfaction was not there. Tragic. [...]

Morgantown, Chestnut Ridge, West Virginia,
July 19, 1939

[…]
Fairfield was hot and the few days that I had planned to spend in the wheat belt shriveled up in the pitiless sun (108°F in the shade from noon to 3 p.m., cooling down at night to a low of 87°F). After a murderous rainstorm, I made a run for it and headed east down the white-hot concrete highway. The air-conditioned room in St. Louis brought a welcome 12-hour night. It was a bit sad to turn my back on the wide, unknown, romantic West. But I have promised myself by all that is holy that it will not be the last time.
[…]
There is so much here that I will always look back upon with nostalgia: the space, the openness, the youthfulness and the ease of living. Sometimes it is so hard to understand why life has to become so difficult, complicated and arduous.

And then there is the other side: my hunger for a deeper dimension, for people who not only *do* things but also can and want to excel by thinking deeply. There is my hunger for music and painting and the secure, settled life. The moist air of August in Holland – the farms among the trees with their little flower gardens – and the dahlias blooming again. […]

Ermelo,
July 11, 1939

My dear son!
Your letter of June 25 from Des Moines with its enclosures is lying in front of me. And it certainly shows that you have had several very difficult weeks to cope with. So I feel the need to send you a few words before you embark and prior to our having the opportunity – hopefully soon – to help you get through this disappointment by discussing it together from much closer by.

Let me say now how thankful I am that you did not change your mind about sending the letter in its present form. Because it is, nonetheless, a very loyal and open testament to what binds us.

And it allows the opportunity – which would have been impossible had you kept silent – to set right what you thought was not correct in Mother's letter. I have not read her letter, and thus must leave open the chance that it could have been misunderstood in places. But when you ask, 'Do you know that in your reply to my letter there was not a single word of rejoicing over what for me would have been such great joy?' then I should like to say straightaway: Mother obviously understood very well that this situation would not bring you happiness but disappointment and heartbreak. And both of us had the impression from your letters about your expectations in California – although we may well have expressed it differently – that Jane would stand by her earlier decision. Naturally, we could not in the least have foreseen that it would take such a markedly different tack. And that is not yet very clear to me either from her two letters; it is a more subtle difference in language than that between English and Dutch that is not clear to me in those letters so now we will just have to wait out the four weeks until we can talk together. I am longing for that more than ever.

[…]

However, while the month of August will be brightened by your return, internationally there are many dark clouds. And I don't like the look of how things are going in our own country either. But we will be able to talk about that soon enough… just like old times.

With a hearty handshake,
Father

PS I have just begun Niebuhr's *Kingdom of God*.

Washington DC,
Sunday, July 30, 1939

[…]

Now that I am here and once again walking the old familiar streets in these final days, I frequently look at myself and wonder: how have you changed? Strange, in Washington everything is still the same: a few new names, the Mellon Gallery almost completed and the New Deal more, much more, under attack than in October. But between the autumn in Washington of that early beginning [...] and the summer heat of today lies a long and wonderful year. [...] The South and the soft, warm winter nights, the appalling poverty, the impoverished land and the denial of rights to the suffering race. So many people come to mind: spirited workers and resigned, beaten-down faces. Chapel Hill and the Resettlement Project in Pandelea. The flat, tropical tidewater, the rolling Piedmont and the mountains. Slums and gullies. Magnificent old mansions and shacks. And then New York, Yale, Boston, Harvard. The gleaming white villages in the valleys of New England, spring in the Connecticut Valley and on the hillsides of Massachusetts. The wide, open spaces between Albany and Detroit. Chicago, the devastated forests in Wisconsin, the lush, green, waving cornfields of Iowa. The slowly withering brown of Kansas. And the long, long concrete ribbon of road heading home, until finally the trusted old car drives over the Arlington Bridge once more, along the Lincoln Memorial, Constitution Avenue, all the big white buildings – Commerce, Labor, Law, I.C.C. and up the Hill, the Capitol. And every step of the way: people, conversations, faces, thoughts, problems. [...]

And by the time this letter arrives in Ermelo, it will all be behind me. Forever?

I can't tell you how much I long for Holland: Ermelo, the house, Jaap, Jochem, Ernst and so many others. And for the sheltered safety of the countryside, the little gardens of the farmers on an August evening and the misty watery light over the polders. For the canals, soon to be adrift with the first yellow leaves of the elms.

Still, I know that you will understand how difficult it is to leave here. I bought for Margote the children's story of Wee Gillis, a young Scotsman who couldn't decide whether he was a Highlander or a Lowlander.[43] Then one day he discovered that he had learned to play the bagpipes so beautifully that he was

---

43. Margote Hausmann, the eldest child of Max's sister Dinah and her husband Herbert, received this book for her birthday. Written by Munro Leaf with illustrations by Robert Lawson, *Wee Gillis* was first printed in 1938 and later became a classic of American children's literature.

welcome in both the Lowlands and the Highlands. Shall I find somebody to teach me to play the bagpipes? And will there be anybody in this time of war to listen to bagpipe players? Or shall I perhaps very soon revert to being just a lowlander once again? I didn't know that there could be room in the human heart for a small, intimate and trusted lowland and a wide, open, new and wild highland at the same time.

Well, for the moment, seven seasick days lie between the two. May the winds be kind to me. [...]

An embrace.

Max

3 John: 13-14 I had many things to write to you, but I am not willing to write them to you with pen and ink; but I hope to see you shortly, and we will speak face to face.

9 781844 010554